Circle of Days

A Church Year Primer
Year B

A celebration of the major themes and texts of the
Christian Year

Paula Franck
Isabel Anders

© 2020 Circle of Days Publishing
https://circleofdayspublishing.com

Cover design by Morgan Kay

ISBN: 9798690129149

In Memoriam

H. King Oehmig
J. H. W. Rhys

"Blessed Lord, who hast caused all holy Scriptures to be written for our learning; grant that we may in such wise hear them, read, mark, learn, and inwardly digest them … " —Archbishop Thomas Cranmer.

Contents

Introduction

Like a great waterwheel, the liturgical year goes on relentlessly irrigating our souls, softening the ground of our hearts, nourishing the soil of our lives until the seed of the Word of God itself begins to grow in us, comes to fruit in us, ripens in us the spiritual journey of a lifetime. So goes the liturgical year through all the days of our lives. —Joan Chittister.

Having spent the last thirty years immersed in the "circle of days" that is the liturgical year—studying, writing, and praying through the many Sundays and Holy Days that make up Years A, B, and C of the Lectionary—we pause to take this moment to reflect on this experience.

One realization that stands out strongly to us is that *reading* and *understanding* are not the same thing, and that the latter takes time and requires many approaches, experiences, and analogies to engender nourishment and growth in our spiritual lives. By offering various perspectives from our tradition and culture to illuminate liturgical Lessons—lines can be drawn, seeming contradictions gentled, and hearts and minds newly challenged. This has happened frequently to us as editors, just as we believe and trust it has with our readers.

Circle of Days as a set of three books will offer theologically based reflections on the Lessons in all three years of the Revised Standard Lectionary. Our purpose is to enable comprehension, comparison, a sense of progression, and especially *heightened experience* of the major events of Jesus' life—the annual Christian Holy Days—within their context in the biblical narrative.

While longer treatments of all the designated Lessons are available (see our *Understanding the Sunday Scriptures,* Years A, B, and C, with H. King Oehmig), in *Circle of Days* we offer the individual worshiper keys to each Sunday's themes in regard to Christian living, to help these Scriptures become more accessible and approachable by prepared hearts and open spirits.

Circle of Days is a "Primer" one can go to first in making ready for Sunday worship and seeking deeper personal understanding. With this in mind, we present the first of the three books: *Circle of Days, Year B*—along with hopes and prayers for the fruits of Scripture to continue to ripen in our readers and in us.

Paula Franck
Isabel Anders

A complete list of all Lectionary Readings can be found in the back of this book.

ADVENT

Advent proclaims that the One who came in humility as a little child will come again in glorious majesty to judge the living and the dead, reminding us that the future as well as the past and the present are in God's hands. — H. King Oehmig.

As the first season of the Church's Liturgical Year, Advent always begins four Sundays before Christmas Day. It is a time of waiting, expectation, hope, and renewal as we prepare for the wonder and mystery of the Incarnation at Christmas. The word advent, from the Latin *adventus,* means coming, and we sense that something extraordinary is about to happen—*will we be ready?*

But along with joyful anticipation, this is also a time of solemn preparation, with Advent's call for repentance and forgiveness. As we watch and wait we are reminded that we live in light of the first Advent of Christ in history, and in expectation of the second Advent in the unknown future. This is a time of "almost and not yet."

Following the pattern of the Lectionary in all three years, the Gospel reading for the first Sunday points to the coming Day of the Lord, with scenes of final judgment at the end of human history. Yet, amid the destruction, believers expect to see God's transforming power to restore creation.

On the second and third Sundays, the focus is always on the dramatic figure of John the Baptist, who prepares the way for the One who is to come.

As Advent comes to an end, the fourth Sunday looks ahead to the celebration of Christmas, as the angel Gabriel brings the news to Mary that she is to bear the Son of God.

The Old Testament readings for this season are customarily taken from the prophets, featuring words of comfort and hope from Isaiah. The Epistle passages challenge the people of God to conduct their lives in ways that will prepare them for the Lord's coming.

This paradoxical wintry season begins with images of final judgment, and ends with the fulfillment of God's promises: with the birth of the Messiah, who will return to bring all the world under his gracious reign.

Advent 1

Our spiritual life depends on his perpetual coming to us, far more than on our going to him. —Evelyn Underhill.

The season of Advent begins with the emphatic warning to "Beware, keep alert" (Mk. 13:33) for the coming of the Son of Man. Today's Gospel passage features dramatic images of what that coming will be like.

In the longest single discourse in Mark, Jesus is responding to a question from his disciples Peter, James, John, and Andrew about Jesus' prediction of the destruction of the temple (13:1-4). He calls for vigilant watching for the coming of the Son of Man. Verses 24-25 draw on Old Testament prophetic tradition to illustrate the cataclysmic nature of events when the Son of Man will come "in clouds" with great power and glory (v. 26; Dan. 7:13-14). Thus Jesus calls for vigilance on the part of all who seek to be the Lord's disciples.

Jesus was aware that his ministry signaled a new intervention of God into the affairs of the world, and he believed that others should be able to perceive it. Thus he compares the signs of the time to a fig tree. Just as the change of seasons can be predicted when the tree puts forth new growth—so, too, do the signs of cosmic collapse and social turmoil foretell that *the coming of the Son of Man is near.*

This is reinforced by the brief parable of a man who leaves his house in the care of his servants when he departs on a journey. At his return he will expect to find everything in good order, with each servant having fulfilled the tasks assigned. The implication is that there will be a severe reckoning if there is evidence of neglect at the owner's unscheduled return. Thus the servants must be prepared always for their master's reappearance.

Likewise, because we cannot know when the Lord will return, we must watch and be alert at all times for his coming. We are to "keep awake" to prepare for this event, living in readiness to receive him. This constant vigilance will lend purpose and direction to our lives.

While the Gospel reading predicts God's climactic intervention in history, the verses from Isaiah begin as an appeal for God to act: "O that you would tear open the heavens and come down ... !" (64:1).

The prophet goes on to describe Israel's past sin and God's just anger. The people perceive themselves as unclean before the Lord—like a "filthy cloth" (v. 6), or a faded leaf that is blown away by the wind. Because of their transgressions, they do not call on the name of the Lord.

Yet there is hope—for despite their failings, the Lord is still acknowledged to be their Father. The people are compared to "clay"—the work of God's hand. As they pray to the Lord for forgiveness, they anticipate God's presence among them.

The Epistle reading expresses themes of expectation and hope as the Corinthians live in anticipation of the return of Jesus. Possessing all of God's spiritual gifts, they are equipped to wait confidently for the "revealing of our Lord Jesus Christ" (1 Cor. 1:7). They affirm that God is faithful. Indeed, it was through God that they were called into the fellowship of Christ Jesus.

Thus Advent is a time not only to anticipate God's new act in creation through the coming of Jesus Christ, but also to celebrate the promise that Christ will return and forever continue his gracious rule.

Christ comes to us in many different ways, and often when we least expect his appearance; thus we are to "keep awake" and watch. During this Advent season, how will you use this time to prepare for the coming of Christ?

Advent 2

The celebration of Advent is possible only to those who are troubled in soul, who know themselves to be poor and imperfect, and who look forward to something greater to come. —Dietrich Bonhoeffer.

Today the compelling figure of John the Baptist takes center stage. With his message of preparation, expectation, and repentance, John is a key figure in our understanding of the season of Advent, playing an important role in all four Gospels. Mark's story begins—not with Jesus, but with John.

John had a successful ministry in his own right with his own disciples. Yet he clearly understood that his primary call was to *prepare the way* for the One to come, who was greater than he.

According to Luke, John was the son of Elizabeth and the priest Zechariah, and was also related to Jesus (Lk. 1:36). John had already been arrested and imprisoned before Jesus began his public ministry; thus there was no contact between the two men after Jesus was baptized by John. John's influence caused Herod the Great's son to have John beheaded. And when Jesus appeared, Herod feared that he might be John the Baptist resurrected.

The opening verse of Mark's Gospel conveys a sense of excitement and anticipation, with the announcement of "the beginning of the good news of Jesus Christ, the Son of God." This bold identification of Jesus as the long-awaited Messiah encapsulates the message of the entire Gospel—as it proclaims the beginning of a new age.

John, as the last of the prophets in the Old Testament tradition, is portrayed as coming out of the wilderness—historically the place not only of testing, but of God's saving acts. John's attire was like that of the Prophet Elijah, whose return was to herald the coming of the Kingdom.

People from throughout Judea and Jerusalem responded to John's call for a "baptism of repentance for the forgiveness of sins." They came to him for renewal as they confessed their sins.

John understood that he served as a witness to proclaim the greatness of the one who would come after him. He saw himself as not even worthy to perform the act of a slave, to "stoop down and untie the thong" of Jesus' sandals. John drew a contrast between his baptism with water and Jesus' Baptism with the Holy Spirit.

Just as John the Baptist prepared the way for Jesus, we can look to John's example in our own work of preparation *to receive the transforming presence of Christ* in our lives.

Isaiah 40:1 expresses themes of expectation and hope: "Comfort, O comfort my people, says your God." The sins of the people are declared forgiven and their penalties paid. In Mark 1:3, John the Baptist echoed the words of Isaiah to "Prepare the way of the Lord, make straight in the desert a highway for our God." Even nature was to respond as the mountains and valleys were leveled and the road made smooth. All this would occur to reveal God's glory to all people.

Our Epistle for today reflects the growing concern that Jesus' return was not going to occur any time soon. "With the Lord one day is like a thousand years, and a thousand years are like one day" (2 Peter 3:8). We are reminded that *it is not for us to know* when the Second Coming is to overtake the world. We cannot expect God to work on our timetable. Our waiting period is a time of self-examination and repentance in order to be prepared to stand before our God.

John the Baptist understood that he was the messenger who prepared the way for the coming of the Messiah. Following his example, what is our role today, especially during this Advent season, in sharing the story of the "good news" of the coming of Christ?

Advent 3

Waiting—that cold, dry period of life when nothing seems to be enough and something else beckons within us—is the grace that Advent comes to bring. —Joan Chittister.

"There was a man sent from God, whose name was John" (Jn. 1:6). Apart from Jesus, no one else is described as having been sent by God, as part of the Divine plan. There are no details here of John's personal background or appearance. He is the prophetic voice—a living presence of God's promise.

John's call was to be a witness to testify to the light. John claims nothing further for himself. John was not the light, but his task was *to enable others to see the light.* "He who comes after me ranks ahead of me because he was before me" (v. 15). Thus when priests and Levites were sent from Jerusalem to question him about his identity, John confessed, "I am not the Messiah." He is instead *a voice calling the faithful to prepare the way of the Lord.*

When the Pharisees asked John why he baptized if he was not the Messiah, Elijah, or the prophet, John replied that he baptized with water, but there was *one whom they did not know* who was far greater. Jesus was misunderstood by many throughout his ministry, including his most intimate followers. John, as the humble and obedient messenger who prepared the way for him, emphasized that *Jesus was the focal point.*

Later, Jesus would say that no one who had lived was more a servant of God than John the Baptist (Mt. 11:11). Yet the person who is least in the Kingdom of heaven, whose light simply reflects the presence of Jesus, is greater than John.

Our responsibility today is to follow the example of John—to live in such a way that our lives manifest and proclaim the light of Christ in the world.

As we reach this halfway point in the weeks of Advent, often referred to as *"Gaudete* Sunday," our Epistle begins by reminding us to "rejoice always" (1 Thess. 5:16). Paul's conclusion to his first letter to the

Thessalonians reflects a sense of expectation as the community anticipates the Second Coming of the Lord. The passage gives specific directions for faithful living so that our "spirit and soul and body be kept sound and blameless at the coming of our Lord Jesus Christ."

With a spirit of joy, the believers were to pray without ceasing, giving thanks for all things according to God's will for them. They were to be fully receptive to the leading of God's Spirit and to heed the words of the prophets. Yet they were also to test whatever came to them in light of the Gospel in order to discern between good and evil.

We, like the Thessalonians, also live in the time between the first and second advents of our Lord. Thus we are challenged to wait and to prepare ourselves as faithful disciples, ready to welcome Christ into our lives.

Isaiah 61 also reflects today's mood of joyful anticipation with a proclamation of the "year of the Lord's favor." The speaker announces that he has been filled with the Spirit of the Lord and anointed to bring good news. Jesus himself used the words of Isaiah (61:1-2) to describe his own call as he began his public ministry (Lk. 4:18-19).

Just as new life comes forth in the spring, so will righteousness and praise to the Lord be made known in all the world.

On this Gaudete *[Rejoice!] Sunday, the readings reflect a sense of joyful trust in the Lord. What gives you cause for rejoicing and thanksgiving as we draw nearer to the light, as described by John the Baptist?*

Advent 4

What must it have been like to walk a way she could hardly perceive, while carrying within herself—in her heart and womb and bones—a light unlike any the world had ever seen? What must it have been like for the archangel who witnessed Mary's yes? —Jan Richardson.

On this final Sunday of Advent, the closing words of the Apostle Paul's letter to the Romans express the hope of the season: "the mystery that was kept secret for long ages" (Rom. 16:25). This mystery was disclosed through the prophetic writings and then also extended to the Gentiles. God's intent from all eternity is now revealed to us, fulfilled in the person of Jesus Christ.

Advent is the opening up of this great mystery and the completion of prophecies made long ago, beginning with God's promise to David of an enduring dynasty.

At the time of today's Old Testament passage, David's kingship is secure. With his foreign enemies defeated and Israel united, David proposes to the Prophet Nathan that he build a permanent home for the Ark of God.

Though the people perceived that God had always moved freely among them and never desired or commanded a house be built, now God promises to construct a house for David; but it will be a house in the sense of *a dynasty.*

David's descendants will continue his kingdom and build a house for the Lord. Thus David's legacy will continue forever. This promise will ultimately be fulfilled with the birth of the Holy Child to Mary, and Christ will be given "the throne of his ancestor David" (Lk. 1:32).

As the Gospel passage begins, the angel Gabriel appears to Mary, a betrothed young woman in the small Galilean village of Nazareth. When the angel greets her as "favored one," she is alarmed; but the angel tells her not to be afraid. He then delivers the startling message that she has been chosen by God to bear a child. This child will be named *Jesus,* which means "God saves." He "will be great, and will be called the Son of the Most High."

In verse 27, Luke has already told us that Mary was betrothed to a man named Joseph, of the house of David. This establishes Jesus' legal connection to the Davidic line, in accordance with the ancient prophecies (2 Sam. 7:12-17). Furthermore, Jesus will rule over Israel (the "house of Jacob") forever, and "of his kingdom there will be no end."

The angel answers Mary's question of how she can conceive a child when she is still a virgin by replying that "the Holy Spirit will come upon you." Thus her child will be holy. While the Gospel of Matthew alludes to the virginity of Mary (Mt. 1:22-23), Luke merely states that Mary is a virgin because she is engaged but not yet married. The focus here is on the miraculous power of God through the Holy Spirit to overcome human limitations.

This theme is further emphasized as Gabriel calls attention to the pregnancy of Mary's cousin Elizabeth, who was thought to be barren and beyond her childbearing years. "For nothing will be impossible with God" (v. 37).

Mary's response—"let it be with me according to your word" (v. 38)—is one of faithful and courageous obedience. In the words of the *Magnificat* (Lk. 1:46-55), Mary gives voice to the wonder and joy of this event and the revolutionary nature of God's Kingdom. Thus future generations will call her *blessed,* for it is through Mary's acceptance of this call that God would bring about the salvation of the world through Jesus Christ.

When the angel gave Mary the startling news that she was to conceive and bear a child who would be the Son of God—what do you think enabled her to accept the Lord's call? What were the challenges and risks, as well as the blessings of her decision? Following the example of Mary, what is God calling you to do?

CHRISTMAS

Christmas is the day that holds all time together.   —Alexander Smith.

The Christmas season begins with the celebration of the Nativity of Our Lord on December 25 and continues for twelve days ending on the Eve of Epiphany or Twelfth Night on January 5. The word Christmas comes from the old English "christmasse" or Christ's Mass. On ancient calendars the celebration was set close to the winter solstice when the days again became longer to reflect the light that Christ brings to the darkness of the world. The date of December 25 was established by the Church in 336.

The same Lessons for the Christmas season are used in all three years of the Lectionary cycle. The promises proclaimed by the prophets are fulfilled with the birth of the Christ Child as told in Luke's familiar nativity story that is always read on Christmas Eve. The mystery of the Incarnation is further explored on the First Sunday After Christmas in the poetic language of the Prologue to John's Gospel, in which we read that "the Word became flesh and lived among us." The season also includes the celebration of Holy Name on January 1 and concludes with portions of Matthew's nativity account on the Second Sunday After Christmas. (Only Luke and Matthew include nativity narratives.)

Most of the Old Testament passages come from the Prophet Isaiah, and are full of expressions of joyful expectation. The Epistles, including Titus, Hebrews, and Galatians, proclaim the salvation brought by the coming of Christ Jesus.

We are filled with joy as we celebrate the birth of God's Messiah, who is Emmanuel—*God with us.* By taking on our human nature and living among us, Jesus is *truly God and truly human* in fulfillment of God's plan for reconciling and redeeming the world. Through Jesus, God's loving forgiveness for all is revealed.

Christmas Day

The Incarnate Word of God comes today, as new as a newborn child, as old and unfailing as eternity. —Susanna Metz.

On this celebration of the Nativity of Our Lord, we find in Isaiah a declaration that "a child has been born for us" (9:6). Isaiah wrote during a time when Israel suffered under foreign oppression, and told of a day when *light would shine* on a world that had lived in deep darkness.

The prophet proclaims that this king in David's line would rule with wisdom as a "Wonderful Counselor." Furthermore, as "Mighty God" he will be an expression of God's power and presence. He will be called "Everlasting Father," caring for the welfare of his people. And as "Prince of Peace" he will bring reconciliation and liberation. His authority will continue to increase, and his reign will lead to endless peace, justice, and righteousness.

Although these proclamations were written in a particular historic context, they later took on messianic overtones as the Christian community saw the salvation proclaimed by Isaiah become a reality in the birth of the Holy Child Jesus.

The familiar words of Luke's narrative announce the circumstances of Jesus' arrival and the nature of his coming reign. Luke sets the birth of Jesus within the political background of the Roman Empire. In contrast to the reign of Augustus Caesar, the birth of Jesus makes manifest the coming of God's Kingdom into the world—not through coercive tactics or displays of power, but by Divine design.

Luke's concerns are theological rather than strictly factual. He sees God's purposes worked out through human events, even when the participants are unaware of their roles. We read that the census sends Mary and Joseph from their home in Nazareth to Bethlehem, the messianic city of David. Joseph's ancestry connects Jesus to David's line, as foretold by the prophets; thus Jesus is of the house of David as well as the only Son of God.

In showing the Holy Family unable to find lodging, Luke introduces the theme of the world's rejection of the Messiah. Here, at the beginning, "the Son of Man has nowhere to lay his head" (Lk. 9:58).

Mary wrapped the child in bands of cloth to keep his bones straight and assure proper growth, and then laid him in the manger. Thus God's Son enters into human life in the most humble of circumstances.

The birth of the Messiah was told first to a group of shepherds, representing the poor and lowly whom Jesus came to serve. Thus the Apostle Paul would later write: "God chose what is weak in the world to shame the strong" (1 Cor. 1:27).

We observe in the narrative how events on earth and in heaven blend together, as an angel of the Lord stands before them, and "the glory of the Lord shone around them." The shepherds are terrified of this glory. However, the angel calms their fears, announcing "good news of great joy" for all people: *In Bethlehem a child has been born who is Savior, Messiah, and Lord.* A heavenly choir also praises God and promises peace to the world.

In Luke, a faithful response to receiving the Good News is to *go out and tell others.* Thus the shepherds become the first evangelists, hastening to see the Christ Child for themselves and then going forth to share this amazing news. Mary herself "treasured all these words and pondered them in her heart."

The words in Titus summarize the message of this Christmas Day celebration: "For the grace of God has appeared, bringing salvation to all" (2:11).

Luke's Nativity Narrative is read every year on Christmas Day. As you read this story again, pay attention to the characters as the events unfold, and reflect on what stands out most vividly for you. In what ways does the miracle of the birth of the Christ Child shape your life of faith?

Christmas 1

In Christ, the Ideal and the Real unite in the Actual. —Alexander Charles Garrett.

The celebration of the Nativity of Our Lord continues with the elegant poetry of the Prologue to the Gospel of John. The Evangelist proclaims that the Word, the *Logos,* became flesh in Jesus of Nazareth. Christ is the agent who gives reality to God's design in creation and links humanity to the Divine. Jesus is our mediator, the *Logos* who was with God and whose purpose he expressed. As the Word, Jesus is the most complete expression and revelation of God.

In the beginning, Wisdom was present with God, and was active in creation. Through Christ *all things came into being.* The Word is the source of light and life for the world. "In him was life, and the life was the light of all people" (1:4).

The contrast between light and darkness in verses 4-5 is a frequent theme in John's Gospel, and recalls the creation of day and night (Gen. 1:3-5). To walk in the light is to choose life; but to walk in darkness is death. The light Jesus brings cannot be overcome by the darkness. John the Baptist was sent to tell the world that *Jesus is the true light* who enlightens all. He proclaims that Jesus "ranks ahead of me because he was before me."

Although the *Logos* brought life to the world, those who were his own failed to receive him (v. 11). There were, however, some who did recognize him and put their trust in him. To them he gave the privilege of becoming children of God. This was not a matter of human ancestry or effort but a product of God's grace.

"And the Word became flesh and lived among us ... " The Word now enters the realm of human history and dwells—literally *pitches his tent*—in our presence. Thus we can realize the grace and truth of God's nature. All of us, disciples then and now, continue to live in the glory that Christ bestows on us. "From his fullness we have all received, grace upon grace" (v. 16).

Through the Incarnation, Jesus became one of us so that we could see, hear, and touch the living Word of God and partake of his fullness. This is the mystery of enfleshing and the miracle of Christmas: the eternal Word taking on full human nature. Thus through the life of Jesus we see God's love for the world as brought by the Son. God not only dwelled with us in the past, but now abides with us in the present through the ordinary moments of our lives.

The Prophet Isaiah rejoiced at the expectation of a new era. A series of oracles in the book proclaim *the restoration of Israel* that the Christian community would later see as *a reflection of God's actions* through Jesus Christ. God's people are compared to a bride and bridegroom clothed with the garments of salvation and righteousness. Just as new life sprouts from the earth, so will the Lord God cause "righteousness and praise to spring up before all the nations" (61:11).

Paul in Galatians describes the Incarnation as the sending of God's Son, who was born of a woman "when the fullness of time had come" (Gal. 4:4). Before Christ came, "we were imprisoned and guarded under the law" (3:23). But Christ has brought reconciliation and new life to believers, who are now heirs with him through his obedience to the will of the Father.

As you reflect on the implications of the Incarnation—God in Christ taking on our full humanity—what is your response to this indwelling presence of God in your life and in the world?

Holy Name

The sweet Name of Jesus produces in us holy thoughts, fills the soul with noble sentiments, strengthens virtue, begets good works, and nourishes pure affections. —St. Bernard.

You will name him Jesus (Lk. 1:31).

Today we focus on the Holy Name of Jesus. Names carry power, and acts done in the name of Jesus can be a reminder of God's presence. The Holy Name feast, eight days after Christmas, was originally called the Feast of the Circumcision, since Luke tells us that on the eighth day Jesus was circumcised and given his name.

According to Mosaic law, three ceremonies are to follow the birth of a male child: circumcision (Lev. 12:3); redemption or dedication of the firstborn (Ex. 13:12-13); and purification of the mother (Lev. 12:2, 4, 6). In the Gospel we read of the purification of Mary and the dedication sacrifice offered for a firstborn child (Lk. 2:22-24).

Through circumcision, the Messiah gains solidarity with humanity and becomes subject to the law—that is, the Messiah is both "born of a woman" and also "born under the law" (Gal. 4:4). However, Luke is more concerned with the naming of Jesus.

In Matthew 1:21, Joseph was told in a dream to name the coming child Jesus, "for he will save his people from their sins." In Hebrew the name Jesus means savior or deliverer. When the angel Gabriel appeared to Mary, Gabriel too declared that the baby was to be called Jesus (Lk. 1:31). Thus, in this naming, Mary and Joseph are obedient to God and follow the requirements of their ancestral faith.

Names in Scripture are often indicators of who an individual is and what that person is called to do. In this way, simple obedience on the part of Mary and Joseph was used for the glory of God, as their child grew up to fulfill his vocation as Savior.

The Feast of the Holy Name reminds us of the salvation Jesus brings to us and to all generations. It is his name that we bless and uphold in our prayers and worship. We affirm that God the Father also hears us, and that we too are sons and daughters of God through Christ our Lord.

The Old Testament reading in Numbers 6 is the priestly benediction, the ancient blessing used in Jerusalem temple worship. Here the Lord instructs Moses to give the words of God's blessing to Aaron and his sons. In this prayer, the Lord's presence, protection, grace, and peace are promised to Israel as God's people.

The concluding line of the reading—"So they shall put my name on the Israelites, and I will bless them" (v. 27)—underscores the relationship between God and Israel. With God's own name bestowed on them, Israel belongs to the Lord.

In Galatians 4, we read that God acted "when the fullness of time had come" to send the Son, born of a woman, to bring salvation. Through Christ we are adopted as God's children; and as heirs to God's Kingdom we now receive the Spirit in our hearts. Thus we can call God by the intimate name of *"Abba!* Father!"

The alternate Epistle reading from the letter to the Philippians calls on the name of Jesus in a "Christ hymn" that eloquently expresses the heart of the Gospel message. In it we are called to have the same mind as Christ—to follow his example of humility and obedience, to the end that "every tongue should confess that Jesus Christ is Lord" (Phil. 2:11).

It is customary to offer our prayers "in the name of Jesus Christ our Lord." What does it mean to pray in the name of Jesus?

Christmas 2

Almighty and everlasting God, the brightness of the faithful souls, who didst bring the Gentiles to thy light, and made known unto them him who is the true light, and the bright and morning star: fill, we beseech thee, the world with thy glory, and show thyself by the abundance of thy light unto all nations through Jesus Christ our Lord. —Gregorian Sacramentary.

Jesus' Nativity story continues with events unique to the Gospel of Matthew (2:13-15, 19-23).

After Jesus' birth in Bethlehem (Mt. 1:18-25), Wise Men, following a star, came from the East seeking the child born king of the Jews. This took place during the reign of King Herod the Great (40–1 B. C.)—a ruthless ruler who dealt harshly with any opposition. Under the pretext of wanting to pay homage to this newborn king of the Jews, Herod told the Wise Men to go to Bethlehem to search for the child and then report back to him.

Thus we read that they followed the star until it came to rest over a house in which they found Mary with the child. Overcome with joy, they worshiped him and offered their gifts of gold, frankincense, and myrrh.

However, as the visitors prepared to leave, they were warned in a dream not to return to King Herod. Always on guard against any threats to his power, Herod intended *not* to worship the child, as he had told the Wise Men, but to gain information in order to destroy a potential usurper.

After the Wise Men left, Joseph was told in a dream by an angel to take his family and flee to Egypt, as the child was in danger from Herod. Realizing that he had been deceived by the Wise Men, Herod ordered all children under two years of age in the area of Bethlehem to be killed (2:16-18).

For Matthew, the sojourn in Egypt was in fulfillment of a prophecy of Hosea (11:1). The words in the Gospel are: "Out of Egypt I have called my son" (2:15).

When Herod died, Joseph again was told in a dream that his family could return to Israel (Mt. 2:20). Joseph was still reluctant to go back to Bethlehem in Judea; therefore, in another dream, he was told to go to Galilee as a safer place. Thus he was guided to the obscure village of Nazareth in Galilee. The perils of the Holy Family reveal that from the beginning Jesus was perceived as a threat to the political and religious establishment that would seek to destroy him.

Just as a providential warning led Joseph and his family away from danger and exile, the words of the Prophet Jeremiah also exemplify God's care and guidance. The prophet had promised that the Lord would gather the people from the ends of the earth and bring them home again (3:9a). God would lead them with fatherly compassion on a level road so none would stumble.

He assured them that the Lord who had scattered Israel would now seek and guard them like a shepherd. Old and young alike would proclaim God's goodness and bounty: mourning would be turned into joy as God gave "gladness for sorrow" (v. 13).

The Epistle to the Ephesians proclaims another aspect of God's care for all humanity. The letter asserts that every spiritual blessing was preordained in heaven before the world's foundation and was made accessible by the Messiah (1:3). God the Father destined believers for adoption as children through Jesus Christ; therefore they have been and are yet being prepared to participate in this glorious destiny.

Jesus' disciples have been rendered blameless before God, and thus are able to be received into God's family. Because of this, they are led to praise this glorious grace that has been freely bestowed through love.

The passages for today focus on faith in God's providential care. How do you experience God's guidance and nurture in your own life?

EPIPHANY

O God, by the leading of a star You manifested Your only Son to the peoples of the earth: Lead us, who know You now by faith, to Your presence, where we may see Your glory face to face. —*Book of Common Prayer.*

The season of Epiphany begins on January 6 with the celebration of the Feast of the Epiphany or the Manifestation of Christ to the Gentiles. This holy day commemorates the visit of the Magi to see the Christ Child as recorded in the Gospel of Matthew. As proclaimed by the prophets and exemplified by the Magi, *the mission of the Church is for all peoples.*

Epiphany comes from a Greek word meaning showing forth, appearance, or manifestation. An epiphany is an experience of transformation and profound grace that reveals something about who God is. Jesus is the revelation of God through whom we see God's glory face to face. Thus during Epiphany the Lectionary focuses on how Christ is revealed in the world and in our lives.

The Epiphany season varies in length from four to nine Sundays—depending on when Lent begins that year. Every year we read an account of the Baptism of Jesus on the First Sunday After the Epiphany. Therefore, during this season we remember our own Baptism and rededicate ourselves to our calling as followers of Jesus. On the Last Sunday of Epiphany the account of the Transfiguration of Jesus is always read—a pivotal revelation of Christ's glory before we begin the journey of Lent.

Year B of the Lectionary cycle features readings from the Gospel of Mark. Thus during Epiphany we encounter passages from Mark's first two chapters that depict the early ministry of Jesus—as he calls his first disciples, teaches, and heals. The Epistles are from 1 and 2 Corinthians; and the Old Testament readings focus on various aspects of God's call.

Christ is the light who shines through the darkness and brings God's grace to all. As we rejoice in this marvelous gift, we are strengthened in our own call to bring the light of Christ to all the world.

The Epiphany

**When one has gone to Bethlehem, a radical change takes place.
—A Monk of the Eastern Church.**

The Epiphany, celebrated on January 6, brings us to the end of the twelve days of Christmas. It is often commemorated as a Feast of Lights, a reminder that Christ is the light of the world.

This image of light coming into the world was proclaimed in Isaiah to describe the exiles' return from the darkness of captivity in Babylon. It was the dawn of a new age, heralding the brilliance of God's glory: "Arise, shine; for your light has come, and the glory of the Lord has risen upon you" (Is. 60:1).

The prophet proclaimed that other nations would be drawn to this light, and kings would come to the "brightness of your dawn." The returning exiles would also be a sign of hope to God's people still dispersed. Isaiah foretold a "multitude of camels" from afar bringing gifts of gold and frankincense. Thus Israel's restoration would draw the world to the true light.

In contrast to the Gospel of Luke (2:1-20), Matthew's nativity story has no journey from Nazareth, and no angels proclaiming the birth of the Messiah to shepherds in fields. Instead, we read that "Jesus was born in Bethlehem of Judea" (Mt. 2:1), the ancestral home of David. Matthew had already established that Jesus was the Messiah, the Son of David (1:1).

The birth is set during the reign of King Herod the Great (40–4 B. C.). Herod was a ruthless ruler who dealt harshly with any opposition, even ordering the execution of his wife and three sons.

Wise Men from the East, often called Magi, traveled to Jerusalem seeking "the child who has been born king of the Jews" (v. 2). They were priests who studied dreams and astrology. In the ancient world, the births and deaths of great figures were believed to be accompanied by celestial phenomena.

Herod, fearing a threat to his authority, was alarmed when he learned that these strangers were seeking another king. Thus he consulted with the chief priests and scribes as to where the Messiah was to be born. They told Herod that the child would come from Bethlehem of Judea (Micah 5:2; 2 Sam. 5:2).

Herod conferred secretly with the men from the East. Under the pretext of also wanting to pay homage to this newborn king, he told them to go to Bethlehem and "search diligently for the child," and bring back word.

Thus the Magi "followed the star" until they found Mary and the child. Overwhelmed with joy, they knelt down and paid him homage, offering gifts of gold, frankincense, and myrrh.

After the Magi had completed their mission, they were warned in a dream not to go back to Herod. Thus they returned to their own country by another way.

A similar warning prompted Joseph to take his family and flee with them beyond Herod's lands. Herod again feared the child; so he ordered the slaughter of all children under two years of age.

Just as the visitation of the Magi reveals the wideness of God's grace, Ephesians declares that now the Gentiles have become "fellow heirs, members of the same body, and sharers in the promise in Christ Jesus through the gospel" (3:6). All are now members of the Body of Christ and can take part in the promises made by God through the Son.

As you reflect on the quest of the Magi to find and worship the Christ Child, what is the significance of their journey for us today? How do you seek to find Christ—the light of the world—revealed in your own life?

Epiphany 1

God looks at us and says, "You are my dear, dear child: I'm delighted with you." —N. T. Wright.

An account of Jesus' Baptism is always read on the First Sunday of Epiphany. At this event, God revealed Jesus as the Beloved Son.

But long before Jesus appeared to John the Baptist, the symbols of water and Spirit were integral to the creation narrative. In the beginning, we read, the earth was a formless void, and "a wind from God swept over the face of the waters" (Gen. 1:2). All was chaos and enshrouded in darkness until the Lord said, "Let there be light." God saw that the light was good and separated it from the darkness on the first day of creation.

According to Romans, when God speaks, it is to call "into existence the things that do not exist" (4:17). Thus the light is brought forth through the power of God's Word to counter the darkness. Both light (Day) and dark (Night) become facets of the order of creation.

The voice and Spirit of the Lord were also present at the Baptism of Jesus. But in this sacramental act, the chaos of the waters at creation is replaced by the promise of salvation in the waters of baptism, signifying a *new* creation.

Mark describes John the Baptist as an Elijah-like figure who came out of the wilderness calling for repentance and baptizing those who came to him. While John baptized with water, the one to come was to baptize with the Holy Spirit (1:8).

It would not seem that Jesus would need to be baptized; yet he came to John and received this cleansing rite in the Jordan River. Jesus had no guilt to wash away; but by this baptism he identified himself with the spiritual needs of humanity. As Jesus came up out of the river, he was empowered by the Holy Spirit.

In the Gospel of John, the Baptist witnesses that he saw the descent of God's Spirit in the form of a dove (Jn. 1:32) as Jesus was being baptized. The other Gospels are less clear as to whether Jesus alone perceived the event, or whether it was also observed by John or others (Mt. 3:13-17; Lk. 3:21-22).

At that moment, Mark maintains that Jesus "saw the heavens torn apart" (v. 10); whereas the accounts of Matthew and Luke say that the heavens were opened. There was a further confirmation of the Divine presence offered at this time. In words that echo Isaiah 42:1 and Psalm 2:7, a "voice from heaven" proclaimed, "You are my Son, the Beloved; with you I am well pleased" (v. 11b). These words will be repeated later on the occasion of Jesus' Transfiguration (Mk. 9:7).

The Baptism of Jesus conveys to us the origin of his identity. Through reading of this experience, we learn that *Jesus knows who he is*. Others will discover this truth through his life and ministry.

The difference between John's baptism with water and Jesus' baptizing with the Holy Spirit is found in the account of Paul's meeting with some disciples in Ephesus. They had been baptized by John, but did not know about the Holy Spirit. Paul explained that John's baptism was for repentance and for proclaiming the one who was to come. Paul then laid hands on them, and they received the Holy Spirit.

We too are empowered for ministry as God's servants by the Holy Spirit through baptism. Along with Jesus, *we are God's beloved* and will be sustained as we continue to do the Spirit's work.

Recall your own baptism, and reflect on what it means for you, especially in light of the fact that Jesus also was baptized. Through the water of baptism, how are you transformed and empowered by the Holy Spirit as God's beloved?

Epiphany 2

God first knows Nathaniel, and, because of God's deep knowledge of him—the type of deep knowledge hinted at in Psalm 139—Nathaniel is able to know Jesus for who he is. —Lauren F. Winner.

Jesus told his disciples, "You did not choose me but I chose you" (Jn. 15:16).

In the Old Testament, the boy Samuel was called to be a prophet. He would later become one of the central figures in Israel. Dedicated to the service of the Lord in gratitude by his mother Hanna (1 Sam. 1:26-28), Samuel served Eli, the priest at Shiloh.

Samuel was called during a time when reports of seeing visions and hearing the word of the Lord were rare. When Samuel heard his name called, the boy assumed that it was Eli and went to his bedside. After the third time, Eli came to the conclusion that the Lord was calling Samuel, and told Samuel to answer: "Speak, Lord, for your servant is listening."

Thus Samuel became the Lord's prophet to all Israel, and it was said that the Lord "let none of his words fall to the ground" (vv. 19-20). The story of Samuel illustrates that hearing and obeying God's call is not dependent on age or a previous relationship with the Lord.

In the Gospel we read how Jesus begins calling his disciples. The brothers Andrew and Simon Peter had already committed themselves to Jesus (Jn. 1:35-42). As Jesus traveled on to Galilee, he saw Philip and invited him to "Follow me" (v. 43). Philip then went to Nathanael to tell him of the one about whom Moses and the prophets wrote: "Jesus son of Joseph from Nazareth" (v. 45). The Messiah was expected to be from David's home of Bethlehem. Thus there would be further attempts to discredit Jesus on the basis of his coming from the insignificant village of Nazareth (Jn. 6:42).

Philip again urged Nathanael to "Come and see" (v. 46). There is no substitute for the direct witness of another believer sharing a personal recognition of Christ as Messiah.

As Nathanael approached, Jesus called him "an Israelite in whom there is no deceit!" When Nathanael asked how Jesus came to know him, Jesus answered that he had seen him under a fig tree. In rabbinic tradition the fig tree, symbolizing peace and security, was a proper place to study the Torah.

Nathanael was incredulous that Jesus could possibly know anything about him, and thus he confessed Jesus as the Son of God and the King of Israel (v. 49). Nathanael's growth from skepticism to faith illustrates the sense of Divine presence that drew people to Jesus, and shows that *confession of Jesus as Messiah* lies at the heart of discipleship.

Jesus then declared that Nathanael would see even greater things: "heaven opened and the angels of God ascending and descending upon the Son of Man" (v. 51). This refers to Jacob's dream at Bethel, in which he saw angels ascending and descending on a ladder (Gen. 28:10-22); and to the "greater things than these" (v. 50) in store for the believer after accepting Jesus' call.

The Apostle Paul tells his Corinthian converts (1 Cor. 6:12-20) that they were sanctified and justified by the Lord Jesus Christ, and warns against dishonorable behavior. No one can earn status with God, so external rules cannot define a person's life.

Since we have been adopted as God's children, our bodies have been made a part of Christ, and therefore are "temples" of the Holy Spirit. Thus we are called to glorify God with our entire being.

Reflecting on the experiences of Samuel, Philip, and Nathanael, how have you been invited into God's service? What are you called to do? How have you been transformed by heeding the Lord's call to "follow me"?

Epiphany 3

We too can be written into God's "story." —Demetrius Dumm.

After Jesus' Baptism and his temptation in the wilderness, Mark mentions the arrest of John the Baptist to mark the shift in focus from John's ministry to that of Jesus. Now in Galilee, Jesus proclaims the good news: God's time has been fulfilled with the coming of Jesus, and in him *the Kingdom of God is at hand.*

The response Jesus calls for in his announcement of this good news is *repentance and belief in the Gospel.* To repent is to turn around, to reorient one's life to God. To believe in the good news is to have faith in *what God has done and now promises to do.*

As the passage continues, the calling of the first disciples illustrates the compelling nature of the good news that Jesus brings, as four fishermen leave everything behind to follow him. First, Jesus calls the brothers Simon and Andrew; and soon thereafter, he calls James and John, the sons of Zebedee. Ordinarily one would not expect commercial fishermen to leave their boats and nets on which their livelihood depended. Nor would the sons of Zebedee leave their father in the care of hired servants—unless they were convinced that Jesus had valid claim on their total lives.

Jesus' call to Andrew and Simon was: "Follow me and I will make you fish for people" (Mk. 1:17). They were being asked to risk, dramatically and suddenly, *everything*—and to take up a completely new profession—one that called for *repentance* and *belief.*

When we receive God's call, we bring to the Lord's service whatever skills and talents we already possess. We also receive new gifts and empowerment. We can only respond to God's call in the moment—and in that response of love, we put our first foot forward on the path of *discipleship*—from which there is no turning back.

In contrast to the immediate and positive response of Peter, Andrew, James, and John to the call of Jesus, Jonah was decidedly reluctant to accept God's call and tried to be as ineffective as possible. In this Old Testament saga, he initially attempted to escape by boarding a ship going in the opposite direction from Nineveh. The story tells how he was caught in a storm at sea, thrown overboard, swallowed by a great fish, and finally "spewed out" (2:10) three days later.

But Jonah was given a second chance. He went to Nineveh—a city so large that it took three days to walk across—and delivered the word of the Lord: "Forty days more, and Nineveh shall be overthrown!" To Jonah's surprise and dismay, the people believed God and repented. Grace prevailed, and lives were saved.

The first letter to the Corinthians deals with issues of marriage and sexual morality. Paul's response to concerns raised by the faith community in Corinth is prompted by an expectation of the immediate return of Christ: "the appointed time has grown short" (7:29).

Because Paul and his followers were convinced that "the present form of this world" was passing away (v. 31), they knew that their lives in the here and now would be determined by *the end that God would bring.*

Paul envisioned a very different community—one that *lived in this world* yet anticipated *another* world. God's promises for the coming age were to be the main consideration as the Corinthians determined how they would conduct their lives in the present.

Jesus' first words in Mark's Gospel are a call for repentance and belief in the good news that "the Kingdom of God is at hand." This proclamation compelled those who heard it to follow Jesus. How does this declaration shape your life of faith and vision for the future?

The Presentation

The people, to show that they carry as it were Christ in their hands, take the blessed candles in their hands. —Ancient saying.

"When the time came for their purification according to the law of Moses, they brought Jesus up to Jerusalem to present him to the Lord" (Lk. 2:22).

Luke's Gospel carefully pointed out that the Holy Family faithfully observed the law or *Torah* as they brought the infant Jesus to the temple forty days after his birth for the traditional rites of presentation and purification.

Jesus had been circumcised on the eighth day (Lk. 2:21) and given the name designated by the angel Gabriel (1:31). According to Mosaic law (Ex.13:1), firstborn male children were to be consecrated as "holy to the Lord" (Lk. 2:23). This was also the occasion for the purification of Mary. After the birth of a son, the mother was to remain homebound until the fortieth day, when she offered a sacrifice at the temple. For those of lesser means such as Mary, an offering of a pair of turtledoves or pigeons was sufficient.

Also present on this day were two figures of great personal piety. One such individual was Simeon, whose devotion had opened him to the presence and guidance of God's Holy Spirit. He had been promised that "You will indeed see the consolation of Israel." Simeon had total trust in that promise and was able to recognize the consolation as *personified in this Child being presented.*

He took the infant in his arms and offered praise to God in the prophetic words that have become known through the ages as the Song of Simeon—the *Nunc Dimittis: I need ask no more of life now that I have seen your salvation. The salvation you have prepared is not for us alone, but for all peoples. In being a light to the Gentiles, your salvation is the glory of your people Israel.*

Simeon anticipated a joyous future when the Holy Child would bring down the powers that were now misleading God's people. But Simeon also warned Mary of sorrow to come. Nonetheless, despite controversy and opposition and the grief that Mary herself would suffer—in the end all would be blessing.

The Prophet Anna, a widow, also resided in the temple, where she had spent most of her life fasting and praying. She in turn would praise the Lord for all that was to be accomplished through this child. Those who would seek redemption needed to look no further. When all that tradition required was accomplished, the Holy Family returned to Galilee, where the child Jesus grew with the favor of God upon him.

So *the Lord came to his temple* as proclaimed by the Prophet Malachi (3:1), who had promised that God would send a messenger to prepare for the Lord's coming. Indeed, the Lord would come suddenly—*as a fire* to melt away the sinfulness that hindered the people from presenting acceptable offerings to God.

The letter to the Hebrews stresses the implications of the Incarnation in the person and work of Christ. Christ's complete sharing of our humanity, our flesh and blood, enabled him to be our champion in setting us free from death. As our High Priest, he presents himself as a sacrifice of atonement to God our Father for the sins of his people (2:17).

Anna and Simeon were models of faith as they prayed and awaited the fulfillment of God's promises. What individuals are examples of faithful discipleship for you? How do they influence your life of faith?

Epiphany 4

Jesus will most likely come to our rescue through another person. Likewise, Jesus will work through you in reaching or rescuing another person who is stuck.   —Curtis Almquist, SSJE.

After Jesus called his first four disciples, he traveled to Capernaum in Galilee, which would become the center of his local ministry. Mark describes a typical day in Jesus' ministry as he goes to teach at the synagogue on the Sabbath.

Local synagogues were the focus of Jewish religious life, and early in his ministry, Jesus often taught in them. However, after his rejection in Nazareth (6:2-6), increased hostility led him to teach his disciples privately or address larger crowds in the open. But here the people in the synagogue are "astounded at his teaching, for he taught them as one having authority, and not as the scribes" (v. 22).

The scribes, along with the elders and chief priests, were among Jesus' most adamant opponents. But while the scribes taught with human authority, Jesus spoke from Divine perspective.

Jesus' authority was further illustrated in an encounter with a man believed to be possessed by a demon or "unclean spirit" (v. 23). *Unclean* is used here to mean *opposed to what is holy* rather than immoral or impure.

First, the disturbed man attempts to resist the Divine power of Jesus as he cries out, "What have you to do with us, Jesus of Nazareth? … I know who you are, the Holy One of God" (v. 24). In Mark, unclean spirits and human outsiders recognize Jesus' identity, while those who might be expected to know Jesus do not.

Jesus at once commands the hostile spirit to be silent and depart from the man. The immediate release the man experiences is accompanied by convulsions and loud cries. Once again the crowd responds with amazement: "What is this? A new teaching—with authority!"

In the ancient Near East, belief in powerful demons was widespread, and exorcisms were not uncommon. In Mark's Gospel, this deliverance is Jesus' first public act of ministry, and dramatically demonstrates the power and authority of his word.

As this day in the ministry of Jesus continued, he healed Simon Peter's mother-in-law of a fever; and by the end of the Sabbath, he had cured many who were sick or possessed. Thus, as his fame spreads throughout Galilee, Jesus becomes widely considered an intriguing figure of power and mystery.

As the passage in Deuteronomy begins, Moses promises the people of Israel that God will "raise up for you a prophet like me" after Moses himself is no longer with them (18:15). He goes on to remind them of the meeting at Mt. Horeb when God spoke to Israel and gave them the Ten Commandments.

He affirms that *all true prophets are called by God,* and it is the Lord who gives them their words. Thus, if the people do not heed them they will be held accountable to God. The early Christian community saw the promise of a prophet like Moses fulfilled in Jesus.

In the first letter to the Corinthians, Paul addresses whether or not Christians were permitted to eat leftover meat from sacrifices to pagan idols. He advises that it is better for those who understand that *idols do not exist* to refrain from eating such meat as an example. However, the real issue here is not meat, but the strength of the community.

It is love that binds the believers together, and concern for others should take precedence over individual preferences. "Knowledge puffs up, but love builds up" (8:1b).

Often in the Gospel of Mark, outsiders such as the man with an "unclean spirit" are the ones who affirm Jesus' identity as the "Holy One of God." How do you recognize and acknowledge the presence of Jesus in your life?

Epiphany 5

When we see lives transformed by Christ, time and again what we see is change so radical, so overwhelming, that you would never guess what had been there before. —Jennifer Fitz.

Following the exorcism of an "unclean spirit" from a man at the synagogue (Mk. 1:21-28), Jesus goes to the home of Simon and Andrew with James and John. When they arrive, Jesus is told that Simon's mother-in-law is ill with a fever, indicating that Simon was married at the time of his call. (1 Cor. 9:5 suggests his wife joined him on some missions.)

When Jesus takes the woman by the hand and raises her up, the fever immediately leaves her. She gets up from her bed and begins serving the household guests. Simon's mother-in-law embodies the ideal of discipleship and foreshadows the actions of the women who later ministered to Jesus at the cross (Mk. 15:41).

The second of three scenes in this passage (vv. 32-34) begins at sunset, at the end of the Sabbath, as people from the surrounding area bring to Jesus those who are sick or have indications of possession. It seems as though the whole city has gathered to anticipate miracles from this man of compassion and power.

The third scene (vv. 35-38) takes place early the next morning as Jesus goes out to a deserted place to pray. Since Jesus' authority comes from God, he seeks time alone to pray and discern God's will. When Simon and the others find him, they say, "Everyone is searching for you."

Jesus replies that it was time to go on to the neighboring towns, "so that I may proclaim the message there also; for that is what I came out to do" (v. 38). Jesus' primary purpose is to broadcast the good news; therefore he was not deterred by the acclamation of the crowds. Afterward he left Capernaum and continued his healing ministry throughout Galilee.

Jesus' constant movement at this time points to the urgency of his words: "The time is fulfilled, and the kingdom of God has come near … " (Mk. 1:15). Although healing and restoring lives is important, this proclamation must take precedence—for it is through the Kingdom that the power of healing is fully manifested.

Epiphany themes of discipleship and manifestations of the power of God are also found in the other readings. In the Old Testament, the Prophet Isaiah proclaims the incomparable greatness and goodness of God.

Chapters 40-55 of Isaiah provide hope and the promise of return to the people of Judah, as well as consolation during their exile in Babylon. The prophet offers reassurance that the Lord has not forsaken the people, and nothing can withstand the power of their God.

The Lord is the everlasting Creator who "does not faint or grow weary" (v. 28c). Thus they are to wait for the Lord until "they shall mount up with wings like eagles" (v. 30).

The focus of Paul's first letter to the Corinthians was to help the community in Corinth overcome their divisions. Paul declares that he has been called to proclaim the Gospel, but has not claimed all his rightful privileges as an Apostle (1 Cor. 9:1-15). However, this is not cause for boasting; this is Paul's *vocation*—he cannot choose *not* to proclaim the Gospel.

Paul also knew that the *externals* of this way of life alone, whether for Jew or Gentile, could not bring anyone to God. But with love as the guiding force, all now are *freed from the law* through Jesus Christ.

Jesus' understanding of his vocation differed from others' expectations, with the proclamation of God's Kingdom taking precedence. As you reflect on your own life and call to God's service, what are your most pressing concerns? What is your part in keeping the Gospel message alive and vibrant in the world today?

Epiphany 6

**When we honestly ask ourselves which person in our lives means
the most to us, we often find that it is those who, instead of giving
advice, solutions, or cures, have chosen rather to share our pain
and touch our wounds with a warm and tender hand. —Henri
Nouwen.**

In Jesus' time, any number of chronic skin diseases might have been
called leprosy, not only what we now call Hansen's Disease. In any case,
those with such skin disorders were subject to a number of social and
religious restrictions.

Chapters 13 and 14 of Leviticus provide specific directions in
regard to such diseases. Lepers were considered "unclean," condemned
to live outside the community. Leprosy was thought to be punishment
for sin; and for an individual to be cured of this dread disease was akin
to being raised from the dead.

As Jesus was traveling throughout Galilee, proclaiming his
message in the synagogues and bringing deliverance, a leper came to him
seeking cleansing (Mk. 1:40). Moved by pity, Jesus reached out his hand
and touched the outcast man, saying, "Be made clean!" (v. 41).
Immediately, the signs of disease disappeared. The leper was not only
cured of his ailment —he was also brought back into the community.
The unnamed man was restored to wholeness in relation to God and
others.

Afterward Jesus sent the man away, sternly warning him not to tell
anyone, and to go to the priest. He was to obey the rules for securing
readmission into community life, becoming certified by the priest and
making the appointed thank-offering. But after the leper told others of
his miraculous cure, Jesus could no longer heal openly. People
understandably came from everywhere seeking similar cures. Thus,
fearing that his miracles would overshadow the proclamation of the
Kingdom—the core of his message to the world—Jesus had to withdraw
from the settled communities.

The Old Testament story of the healing of the Syrian army commander Naaman relates how a young Israelite slave girl wished to see him freed from his disease. Thus she told her mistress, Naaman's wife, of a powerful prophet in Israel. If Naaman would go to this prophet, he would surely be healed.

Naaman went to the king of Aram, who wrote to the king of Israel requesting healing for Naaman. Soon Naaman arrived in Israel with a full entourage and elaborate gifts. But the king of Israel was greatly distressed, fearing this impossible request could lead to war. However, when Elisha heard about it, he saw an opportunity to establish his own authority and reveal God's glory.

Elisha sent a messenger who told Namaan to bathe seven times in the Jordan River. Naaman thought that surely one of the rivers of his own country would be more effective. But as he turned away in anger, his servants persuaded him to do as Elisha had commanded.

Naaman carried out the command, and found that he was cured. In joy he went before Elisha and declared, "Now I know that there is no God in all the earth except in Israel" (2 Ki. 5:15b).

The Apostle Paul in 1 Corinthians speaks of a foot race in which only one can be declared the winner. However, for God's athletes there is more to be won than a perishable crown of leaves. Instead, there is an imperishable crown of salvation.

The spiritual quest is not against a rival, but with one's self. Thus, in order to achieve this goal, we must act with purpose. Christ gave his life for others, making way for the blessings of the Gospel—as we discipline our lives in order to serve one another.

We read the stories of two men who were cured of the disease of leprosy. No longer outcasts, they were also healed—made whole again—and could rejoin their communities. How do you experience the healing power of Jesus in your life?

Epiphany 7

In our society forgiveness is often seen as weakness. People who forgive those who have hurt them or their family are made to look as if they really don't care about their loved ones. But forgiveness is tremendous strength. It is the action of someone who refuses to be consumed by hatred and revenge. —Sister Helen Prejean.

In the face of exile and destruction, the Prophet Isaiah proclaimed that God was "about to do a new thing ... " (43:19). Isaiah perceived that God was even then preparing for the return of the exiles from captivity in Babylon. God would forgive Israel because it is God's nature always to be faithful and forgiving.

This compassionate forgiveness is fully manifested in Christ Jesus. Increasingly, Jesus is being revealed as one who speaks with authority as he heals many people of their infirmities. All of his faithful actions inspire awe from the crowds. However, now his ministry also begins to evoke controversy and opposition.

As the power and reputation of Jesus grew, large crowds of people gathered around him. In today's passage, so many had crowded around the house where Jesus was staying in Capernaum that there was no room inside—not even around the front door.

When four men arrive carrying a paralyzed man on a mat, they cannot get through the crowd to bring the man to Jesus. Houses in Palestine often had a flight of steps built on the outside that led to the roof. Not to be daunted by the crowd, the men make a hole in the roof (most likely composed of mud and thatch) and lower the man into the room below.

Impressed by the faith of the paralytic man's friends, Jesus responds with the shocking statement, "Son, your sins are forgiven" (Mk.1: 5). God is the source of the forgiveness; but Jesus is the one who *declares the pardon.*

However, to the scribes present who hear this pronouncement, Jesus' words amount to blasphemy, since only God can forgive sins (Ex.

34:6-7). In the eyes of the law, forgiveness of sins required confession, a change of heart, and often a sacrifice. Blasphemy was punishable by death (Lev. 24:16); and in Mark's Gospel, this was the charge ultimately used to condemn Jesus.

Jesus asks the scribes whether it is easier to forgive the man's sins or to heal his affliction. The scribes are now caught in a dilemma. Since illness was believed to be the result of sin (Jn. 5:14; 9:2), *if the illness is cured, then the sin is also forgiven.* However, there is no evidence of forgiveness; so here the cure of the ailing man *would* be evidence of Jesus' true authority.

Jesus then tells the paralytic man to stand up, take his mat, and go home—since "the Son of Man has authority on earth to forgive sins" (v. 10). The man immediately stands up and goes on his way. Those who witness this miracle are amazed and glorify God.

This same power of God *through Jesus* is proclaimed by Paul as he writes to the Corinthians that Jesus Christ is indeed the "yes" and "Amen" to all of God's promises. Paul in his own experience fully grasped the truth about the *forgiveness* that Christ brings.

He wants the Corinthians (2 Cor. 1) to know that just as God is faithful, *so has Paul been faithful* in his own dealings with them. Therefore Paul can declare in full confidence that all the promises of God have been fulfilled in Christ Jesus, who brings forgiveness and wholeness.

Jesus' authority to forgive sins takes precedence over his power to heal—the "yes" and "Amen" to all of God's promises as expressed by Paul. How do you experience forgiveness through Christ in your life? How does the fact that you are forgiven enable you to forgive others?

Epiphany 8

Jesus loved sinners. He did not just make them objects of love. He saw something he liked in them. That is why their human dignity was restored.   —Krister Stendahl.

In today's Gospel, Jesus invites criticism by calling Levi, the tax collector, and then going to dinner at the house of this unacceptable man. There Jesus and his disciples mingle with other tax collectors and "sinners"—which scandalizes the scribes and Pharisees.

When they ask why he chooses to mingle with such lowlife, he responds: "Those who are well have no need of a physician, but those who are sick; I have come to call not the righteous but sinners" (Mk. 2:17).

While the Pharisees fasted on Mondays and Thursdays, Jesus makes no such demands on his own disciples. Yet when others ask what sort of devotion he *does* require, Jesus answers: "The wedding guests cannot fast while the bridegroom is with them, can they?"

Fasting was universally understood to be inappropriate at a joyous celebration such as a wedding. Yet Jesus warned, "The days will come when the bridegroom is taken away from them, and then they will fast on that day" (v. 20).

The disruption Jesus was bringing would be resisted by many if not most. Eventually the "bridegroom" would be taken forcibly from the disciples. At that time, they would have reason to fast.

Jesus uses metaphors of cloaks and wineskins to make his point: "No one sews a piece of unshrunk cloth onto an old cloak; otherwise the patch pulls away from it, the new from the old, and a worse tear is made. And no one puts new wine into old wineskins"—or the wine will burst out of them. Then "the wine is lost, and so are the skins; but one puts new wine into fresh wineskins" (vv. 21-22).

In their fasting, the disciples were to testify that Jesus' coming was indeed God's new act. It was far more than patching over the lapses that had occurred in the nation's history. And it was not an attempt to hold the new life within the old limits. New wine always calls for new containment that can expand with its explosive development. Such was to be the spread and impact of the Kingdom Jesus heralded.

The Old Testament Lesson from the Prophet Hosea proclaims a new relationship to God. The prophet has announced that Israel, as a nation, is like an unfaithful wife who will be punished for her infidelity. Yet afterward, God will call her back and restore her (2:14-15). In a renewed wilderness experience, as in the earlier entry into the Promised Land, she shall have vineyards and plowland, and reason to sing of God as "my husband."

Covenant and promise have always been God's offering to those who were to be the chosen people. For a redeemed Israel, there would be a New Covenant. Beast and bird and creeping creatures would enhance the life of God's people; and in an age of universal safety, the weapons of war would disappear.

The Apostle Paul writes (2 Cor. 3) somewhat in defense to the Corinthians, apparently after having been accused of commending himself to them. He points out that they, the people themselves, are "our letter, written on our hearts," *a letter of Christ in living flesh.* "Not on tablets of stone"—reminiscent of the Commandments—but on the hearts of believers.

Any gift that Paul has comes through God, who has made him competent as a minister of this New Covenant—not of the letter, but of life-giving spirit.

God is doing a new thing through Christ, and like new wine it must have fresh wineskins. What new things is God doing in your life and in the world? What" old things" do you need to cast aside in order to embrace the transformations of Jesus' incoming Kingdom? How will this change your relationship with others and with God?

Last Epiphany

Occasionally in life there are those moments of unutterable fulfillment which cannot be completely explained by those symbols called words. Their meanings can only be articulated by the inaudible language of the heart. —Martin Luther King, Jr.

Jesus is aware that his ministry will be denounced and rejected, and that he himself will be put to death. Thus his disciples must be prepared for that eventuality and made aware that *there is a glory that death cannot suppress.*

And so Jesus takes Peter, James, and John up a high mountain, which will offer them both privacy and a symbolic closeness to God. The sense of mystery and awe is heightened as Jesus becomes "transfigured" before them: " ... his clothes became dazzling white, such as no one on earth could bleach them" (9:3).

Appearing with Jesus are two figures from Israel's past: Elijah, considered first among the prophets; and Moses the lawgiver. They point to Jesus as the one who fulfills the law and the prophets. Both were faithful leaders who faced rejection because of their fidelity to God.

The disciples are overwhelmed by this blinding display of God's glory—they are terrified and speechless. In their confusion, Peter proposes that they build booths for Jesus, Elijah, and Moses—similar to those constructed during harvest festivals—to prolong this extraordinary experience.

They are then overshadowed by a cloud, a manifestation of Divine presence. With words that recall the Baptism of Jesus (Mk. 1:9-11), they are told: "This is my Son, the Beloved, listen to him!" They learn that Jesus is going to Jerusalem, where he will be killed by the authorities and raised by God.

The vision leaves them, and Jesus is once more alone with his disciples. As they come down from the mountain, Jesus commands them to tell no one about what they have seen until after the Son of Man has risen from the dead.

The Old Testament account of the departure of the Prophet Elijah is another manifestation of God's glory. Earlier Elijah had called Elisha to be his successor (1 Ki. 19:19). As Elijah's ministry comes to an end, Elisha accompanies him as he travels to visit the companies of prophets. Throughout their journey, Elijah tells Elisha to remain behind. But each time Elisha refuses to leave him (2 Ki. 2:2, 4, 6).

The journey takes them further into the wilderness. At the River Jordan, Elijah strikes the water with his rolled-up mantle, causing the waters to part so that he and Elisha can cross on dry land—just as Moses had parted the waters of the Red Sea with his staff (Ex. 14:21).

When Elijah asks Elisha what he can do for him, Elisha requests to "inherit a double share" of Elijah's spirit, as Elijah's true successor. Elijah promises to grant this request if Elisha sees him as he is taken up to God.

As he envisions a fiery chariot descending and sweeping Elijah up in a whirlwind, Elisha tears his clothing in grief at the departure of his friend and mentor. He then picks up Elijah's mantle, the symbol of Elijah's power, and parts the waters of the Jordan himself—confirming that he is Elijah's successor.

In today's Epistle, the Apostle Paul reminds the Corinthians of "the glory of God in the face of Jesus Christ" (2 Cor. 4:6). This glory is manifested in the Transfiguration of Jesus that is always read on the last Sunday of Epiphany—giving us a foretaste of Resurrection as we anticipate the beginning of Lent.

The Transfiguration of Jesus provides a glimpse of God's glory and a vision of the future to sustain the disciples. When have you been aware of the Divine presence in your own life? How do these experiences continue to provide inspiration and deepen your faith?

LENT

Lent is a time for discipline, for confession, for honesty, not because God is mean or fault-finding or finger-pointing but because [God] wants us to know the joy of being cleaned out, ready for all the good things [God] now has in store.   —N. T. Wright.

The word Lent comes from the Anglo-Saxon word "lecten," which refers to the time of year when the days grow longer. The forty days of this penitential season (excluding Sundays) are a time of self-examination, prayer, and reflection on Holy Scripture. Historically, Lent was a period of preparation for baptism on Easter and recalls the forty days Jesus spent in the wilderness.

Lent begins on Ash Wednesday with the same readings appointed for all three years of the Lectionary cycle, and ends on the Saturday before Easter (Holy Saturday). The First Sunday in Lent is always an account of the temptations of Jesus in the wilderness. The Gospel readings for this year are from Mark and John, in which Jesus explains to his disciples *what it means to follow him.* The Old Testament passages feature God's covenantal relationship with Israel. The Epistles remind us of the salvation brought through Christ's death and Resurrection.

During Holy Week we live out the events that lead up to the suffering and death of Jesus on the cross. The Sunday of the Passion or Palm Sunday begins with the joyous arrival of Jesus in Jerusalem, and ends, in accord with the focus of Year B, with Mark's account of Jesus' crucifixion and death.

The last three days of Holy Week are often referred to as the Triduum. Maundy Thursday comes from the Latin *mandatum,* or command, referring to the two commands Jesus gave his disciples at the Last Supper: to celebrate the Eucharist and to love and serve one another. As we commemorate the crucifixion on Good Friday, the Passion is always read from the Gospel of John. Holy Saturday is a day of rest in anticipation of Easter Day.

During this most solemn season of the Church Year, we follow the example of Jesus as he prepared for his earthly ministry with fasting and prayer. Lent provides time for reflection and renewed commitment to spiritual practices, enabling us to live more fully into new life—to make "room" for God and to examine who God is calling us to be.

Ash Wednesday

Let the mark, the grit, the oil, the feel of another's finger on our brow help us look without fear at our mortality. Let the reminder that we are being transformed from glory to glory by God's love and promise of resurrection help us face who and what we are. —Susanna Metz.

The season of Lent begins with the familiar words: "Remember that you are dust, and to dust you shall return." Although they are a traditional symbol of grief, mourning, and sinful mortality, the ashes of Ash Wednesday also remind us of the redemptive power of God's grace through the Resurrection.

In the Old Testament, the Prophet Joel calls for God's people to repent with fasting, mourning, and weeping (2:1b). The penitents are, in true contrition, to rend their hearts and not their clothing (v. 13a).

The prophet calls the entire community to gather in a solemn assembly, as priests and ministers pray to the Lord, "Spare your people" (v. 17). The book ends with God's Spirit being poured out on all people, as Judah is forgiven and its enemies destroyed.

In our Epistle, the Apostle Paul calls the Corinthians to "be reconciled to God" (2 Cor. 5:20b). Although there is no threat of impending doom hanging over Corinth, as there was in Joel, Paul also conveys a sense of urgency.

As Paul's leadership is called into question, he focuses on what God has done in Christ, the sinless one, to bring the community together. Jesus claimed our sin for his own so that we might become the very righteousness of God (5:21). In being reconciled to God, the Corinthians are to be reconciled with one another, and with Paul as well.

Paul has endured and persevered through affliction, persecutions, and numerous other hardships (6:5). Thus he demands of everyone purity, knowledge, patience, kindness, truth, and love, so that ultimately they may possess everything.

In the Sermon on the Mount, Jesus warns against doing the right things for the wrong reasons. The traditional acts of Jewish religious obligation—almsgiving, fasting, and prayer—are integral to our relationship with God and are not to become public demonstrations. Those who perform pious acts in private will receive their reward from the Father.

Jesus' teachings on these three practices begin with a negative example of the behavior of hypocrites, followed by the proper fulfillment, and ending with the promise of God's reward.

The religious obligation to give to the poor was rooted in the tradition of the Torah (Dt. 15:10-11); but Jesus calls to account the hypocrites who give with great fanfare—"sound a trumpet" (Mt. 6:2)—in order to be praised by anyone.

In regard to prayer, Jesus cites those who "love to stand and pray in the synagogues and at the street corners" (v. 5). Such prayers may gain human recognition; but prayer is essentially about *our relationship with God.*

In the third example, Jesus teaches that those who fast should not draw attention to themselves by disfiguring their faces (v. 16). Fasting was a part of the Jewish tradition of showing humility before God. But again, its purpose was not to win the approval of others, but to remind us that *all our needs ultimately are met by God.*

The passage ends with a reminder that the amassing of earthly goods to indicate an individual's worth is futile, since such material possessions can be wiped out or stolen. But our true worth is in heaven and cannot be destroyed: "for where your treasure is, there your heart will be also" (v. 21).

As we begin our Lenten journey, we are called to the practices of self-examination and prayer. How will you use this time to prepare spiritually for the miracle of Easter? What will your prayer be for this season?

Lent 1

It's a humble journey, a humble journey with Jesus that we begin in Mark's Gospel today, this First Sunday in Lent. It's a quiet, unassuming, modest journey. At the same time it's an amazing, remarkable, life-changing journey. —Susan Gamelin.

The journey of Lent always begins with the testing of Jesus in the wilderness. Mark's version, as read in Year B, is typically brief; thus the passage for today also includes the Baptism of Jesus.

When John baptizes Jesus in the Jordan River, Jesus hears the Divine voice echoing the description of Second Isaiah's Suffering Servant (42:1): "You are my Son, the Beloved; with you I am well pleased" (Mk. 1:11).

The Holy Spirit's descending on Jesus "like a dove" (v. 10b) recalls the image of the Spirit of God that hovered over the waters of creation (Gen. 1:1-2). This Spirit remained with Jesus throughout his ministry.

But following his Baptism, that same Spirit *"immediately drove him out into the wilderness"* (v. 12) for forty days. The wilderness was a place of testing and preparation for a call—for revelation. This passage is reminiscent of Moses' fasting on Mt. Sinai as he received the law (Dt. 9:18); Elijah's time near Mt. Horeb (1 Ki. 19:8); and the forty years that the nation of Israel wandered in the desert (Dt. 8:2).

Mark tells us that here Jesus was "tempted by Satan" (v. 13). In the Old Testament, Satan was seen as the adversary who tested the faithfulness of the chosen (Job 1:6-12). He was one of God's angels, though not one in direct opposition to God. However, by the time of the New Testament, Satan had become identified with evil forces working against God.

Jesus was not alone in the desert; wild beasts appeared. Although peaceful coexistence with animals began at creation (Gen. 1:28; 2:19-20), and was included in Isaiah's promise of a new creation (Is. 11:6-9), wild animals signified danger. But Jesus was unharmed by these beasts, and had angels to wait on him (see Ps. 91:11-13).

When the time of testing was over, the wilderness would become a place for Jesus to find respite from the crowds—a retreat where God was present with him in prayer (Mk. 1:35).

Thus Jesus survived temptation with an understanding of his call as God's chosen servant. Now that John the Baptist had been arrested (v. 14), it was time for Jesus to take up his vocation—to proclaim, in his first spoken words in Mark's Gospel: "The time is fulfilled, and the kingdom of God has come near: repent, and believe in the good news" (v. 15).

In the Old Testament account of God's covenant with Noah after the great flood, Noah and his family are preserved from a worldwide disaster through God's compassion.

Yet even a majority of sinful people were not enough reason for God to destroy the earth totally. And after the flood waters had receded, there was initiated a Divine covenant between Noah and his family and with "every living creature … for all future generations" (Gen. 9:12). Offering a visible sign, God promised to "set my bow in the clouds" (v. 13) as a reminder.

The Epistle in 1 Peter 3 connects the experience of Noah and the flood to the salvation of baptism. Just as the rainbow after the great flood was seen as a sign to Noah of God's faithfulness, the water of baptism serves as a symbol of the new covenant through the death and Resurrection of Christ. Being put to death physically, Jesus gives spiritual life to all.

Jesus' experience in the wilderness is a reminder that we all face temptations and trials. Reflect on times of struggle in your own life. How did these experiences contribute to your life of faith? What were your sources of strength and support?

Lent 2

By loving us first, God makes it possible for us to love others, and Jesus asks only that we share that love. But in so doing he tells us that we must take up our cross and follow him. —Robert L'Esperance, SSJE.

The readings for this second Sunday in Lent challenge us to live in radical faith and belief in God's promises, which are worked out in seemingly impossible ways.

In the Old Testament story, God makes a promise to the patriarch Abram and his wife Sarai. Previously, Noah had been promised that never again would the world be destroyed by a flood (Gen. 9:8-17). This was a covenant with all humanity even to future generations. But now Abram and his family are called to carry out God's redemptive purposes in the world as *the bearers of a new creation.*

This new covenant will extend to Abram's descendants "throughout their generations" (v. 7). As an indication of this profound change in Abram's identity, he will now be called *Abraham,* or "father of multitudes."

Just as Abraham was to be father to the nations, his wife Sarai is to be called *Sarah,* or "princess"; and, no longer barren, she will be blessed with the birth of a son who will insure God's promises.

The Apostle Paul in his letter to the Romans would later refer to this outcome as evidence of Abraham's exemplary faith. Paul explains that the covenant with Abraham depended on "righteousness of faith" (4:13) rather than obedience to the law.

"Hoping against hope," Abraham became the father of many nations, and he "grew strong in his faith as he gave glory to God" (4:20).

This same saving righteousness, Paul asserts, is also granted to those who believe in God as *the one who raised Jesus from the dead.* For what is most important here is not Abraham's faith, but God's faithfulness. We are to value most *what God has done in Christ Jesus,* who suffered death for our sins and was "raised for our justification" (v. 25).

In the Gospel passage, Jesus calls his disciples to radical faith and seeks to help them understand the Messiah's true nature and mission.

Earlier Jesus had clarified his purposes to the disciples: He was to suffer many things, be rejected by the authorities, be killed, and "after three days rise again" (8:31). Jesus stated this quite clearly, but the disciples failed to comprehend.

They expected the Messiah to be a new David who would overcome the nation's enemies, enlarge Israel, and establish justice for God's people. But Jesus tells them that he is destined for an execution, not a coronation—and that they should prepare to *participate in his suffering.*

Peter, who had just proclaimed that Jesus was the Messiah (8:29), took Jesus aside and privately reproached him. Jesus then rebuked Peter in front of all the other disciples for thinking on human rather than Divine things. For Jesus, Peter's efforts to dissuade him from his course are comparable to a message of evil, as he exclaims, "Get behind me, Satan!"

Jesus then tells all those present that if they would follow him, they must "deny themselves and take up their cross" (v. 34). Jesus himself prepared to embrace a criminal's death in obedience to his vocation. Those who are ashamed of his seeming defeat on the cross and would turn away from it are warned that the Son of Man would *then be ashamed to acknowledge them* when "he comes in the glory of his Father" (v. 38).

True believers are those who are willing to follow Jesus by denying selfish aims—ready to lose their lives in the world and take up the cross.

Throughout the season of Lent, the image of the cross is ever before us. What does it mean for you to take up the cross in order to follow Jesus?

Lent 3

Jesus founded on earth a new type of community, and in it and through him *love*—God-given *agape* love—came down to live with power on earth. —Dallas Willard.

While Jesus emphasized the importance of God's commandments (Mt. 5:17-19), he called for more than external compliance. The story of the cleansing of the temple is found in all four Gospels. In John's account, it takes place at Passover, early in Jesus' ministry, immediately following the wedding at Cana (Jn. 2:1-11). In this challenge to the authorities, he called for a true change of heart that would reveal to the world a new way of living.

The temple at Jerusalem was vital in the religious life of the Jewish community. Following the return from the exile, the building of a new temple enabled the resumption of sacrifices in obedience to God. The moneychangers performed a needed service at the temple. Roman coins with pagan images were unacceptable for paying the temple tax and buying sacrificial animals, and had to be exchanged for Palestinian shekels. However, this system made a mockery of the worshipful atmosphere of the temple.

Thus Jesus acted. Taking a whip, he drove the livestock and their owners out of the temple, overturning tables and spilling the coin boxes. "Take these things out of here! Stop making my Father's house a marketplace!" (Jn. 2:16). Thus John portrays Jesus as knowing early in his ministry that *he was indeed the Son of God*. Jesus' actions prompted his disciples to recall a verse from Psalm 69:9: "Zeal for your house will consume me" (v. 17).

When the Jews demanded to know by whose authority Jesus had acted as he did, Jesus replied, "Destroy this temple, and in three days I will raise it up" (v. 19). The crowd heard Jesus' response on a literal level, and these words would later be used against him at his trial. How could he raise up in three days a temple that had been under construction for forty-six years?

John makes clear that Jesus is the true dwelling place of God—that it would no longer be an edifice of lifeless stones and timbers. It would be a *living* structure, the mystical Body of Christ. Later, the disciples would remember and believe his words in light of the Resurrection.

In the first chapter of 1 Corinthians, Paul writes of the seeming foolishness of preaching Christ crucified—a stumbling block to the Jews who demand signs, and folly to the Gentiles, who desire wisdom. However, the Cross, which brings salvation, is the very wisdom of God that the world refuses to accept. God's "weakness" or failure is stronger than human strength.

The Commandments or Decalogue ("the Ten Words"), the heart of the covenant God made with Israel at Sinai (Ex. 20), provided the norms essential for *a unified nation,* and served as the people's ethical and moral foundation. The first set of Commandments defined Israel's relationship with God; warned against idolatry and blasphemy; and commanded a Day of Rest.

The remaining Commandments are concerned with human relationships and living together in community. Parents are to be respected and cared for. The values of human life and peace within the community are to be protected; thus murder, adultery, and theft are prohibited. The injunction against killing refers specifically to murder, since there are actions in the Torah for which the required punishment is death (Ex. 21:12-17).

The command prohibiting false witness against a neighbor involves more than legal perjury; no one should say anything to discredit another. Finally, community members should not covet or desire anything that belongs to someone else. By our keeping these Commandments, God is glorified.

Throughout his ministry, Jesus acted against injustice and invited his followers to experience changed hearts and a new way of living. Called to love God and neighbor, how can you foster peace and justice in your own community?

Lent 4

Throughout the Gospel, Jesus reveals his identity through the many signs he accomplishes (turning water to wine, healing the blind man, raising Lazarus). And now, as he journeys through the final days before Passover, in and out of the city, toward the cross, he reveals an even deeper level of identity. —Dirk G. Lange.

As we continue our Lenten journey, today's readings point to the Passion as a reminder of our need for repentance and forgiveness.

The Book of Numbers recalls the years that the Hebrews wandered in the wilderness following the exodus from Egypt. This was not a glorious journey to the land of promise in Canaan, but a period of discontent over the lack of food and water; conflict over the leadership of Moses and Aaron; and rebellion against God.

Later, the life-saving manna would be remembered as the "bread of angels" (Ps. 78:25); but here it is referred to as "miserable food." The people, impatient because of delays and a detour around the hostile territory of Edom, had lost sight of their original vision of freedom, and felt they had been led into the desert to perish (Num. 21:5).

When "poisonous serpents" (v. 6) bit the people and caused them to die, the Israelites acknowledged their sin, repented, and implored Moses to pray to the Lord to make the snakes, understood as punishment, go away.

God answered Moses' prayer by guiding him to create a bronze serpent on a pole for the people to look up to as they sought relief from the deadly poison of the snakes. Those who had been bitten were to gaze on the bronze serpent and *live*.

In the Gospel for today Jesus, in his conversation with Nicodemus (Jn. 3:1-21), compares the raising of the serpent in the wilderness to his own being raised. Both are indicators of remedies for sin, and both require a response of faith.

As Moses lifted up the serpent in the wilderness, *so must the Son of Man be lifted up on the cross* (see Jn. 8:28; 12:32-33). Both of these acts are signs of God's protecting love and mercy. This is the first Passion prediction in the Gospel of John, early in Jesus' ministry (3:14). Whoever looks to the Cross trusts the outpouring of God's love that leads to eternal life. Jesus foresaw that when he was lifted up from the earth he would be enabled to *draw everyone to himself.*

The Son came *to save* and not to condemn the world. Those who do not believe condemn themselves by their own unbelief. Turning to Jesus is a choice freely offered, and the decision one makes then becomes manifested in deeds.

This passage presents a number of contrasts to make its point: faith and disbelief; life and death; salvation and condemnation; light and darkness; good and evil. We find redemption through belief in *the Son sent by God,* who brings salvation and eternal life.

The Epistle reading also reminds us that God forgives and restores despite human sinfulness and lack of faith in the Divine mercy—"by grace you have been saved" (Eph. 2:5).

Freed from our sins, we are now brought to new life and raised with Christ. Thus we become instruments for the doing of God's will. This is not a matter for boasting or pride. *God's saving grace is a gift* that has been freely given through Jesus, leading to the way of life God intended for us—"created in Christ Jesus for good works … " (v. 10).

As we come to the midpoint of our Lenten journey, today's readings are a reminder of God's infinite mercy and salvation. How do you experience this saving grace of Christ in your life?

Lent 5

There will always be many who love Christ's heavenly kingdom, but few who will bear his cross. Jesus has many who desire consolation, but few who care for adversity. He finds many to share his table, but few who will join him in fasting. Many are eager to be happy with him; few wish to suffer anything for him. Many will follow him as far as the breaking of bread, but few will remain to drink from his passion. —Thomas à Kempis.

It was the Feast of Passover, and Jesus had entered Jerusalem, to the acclaim of many (Jn. 12:12-15). Pilgrims had come to the festival from around the world, including some Greeks, who asked the Apostle Philip if they might see Jesus. *This is the sign that Jesus' ministry is to extend beyond the existing covenant with Israel.*

Up to now, Jesus had insisted that his hour of *fulfilling the will of the Father* had not yet come (2:4; 7:30; 8:20). The religious authorities had resolved to destroy him—especially after the raising of Lazarus caused many to believe in him (11:28-57). But now *the hour for the glorification of the Son of Man has come,* and will be realized *through his suffering.*

Just as a kernel of wheat produces fruit when it dies (12:24), so must Jesus lay down his own life for *the redemption of the world.* Whoever would serve Jesus must follow him even unto death. The servant who does so shall be *where Jesus is* and receive honor from the Father.

John's Gospel does not include Jesus' prayer of agony in the garden on the night before he died. Instead, John places here the question of whether Jesus might be spared the final demand of his vocation. "Now my soul is troubled." Yet Jesus concludes: "It is for this reason that I have come to this hour." He ends his prayer with "Father, glorify your name" (v. 28).

John describes a voice from heaven declaring that the Father *has* glorified Jesus' name, and is about to do so again. At this moment, some people think they hear thunder, while others say an angel has spoken.

Jesus did not need such confirmation, but it assures those present that God has responded.

When Jesus is lifted up on the cross, the fullness of God's love will be made visible, and Satan, the "ruler of this world," defeated (v. 31). Only in this way will Jesus powerfully draw all of rebellious humanity to himself.

The author of Hebrews explains the extent of God's salvation in Christ, who as our great high priest mediates a new covenant through his sacrifice. Previous high priests called by God offered sacrifices for sins—their own as well as those of others.

With Jesus it is different. He did not *choose* his vocation; in the Father's plan he is *both God's Son and a priest forever.* Yet Jesus is also one of us, full of compassion for humanity, for: "Although he was a Son, he learned obedience through what he suffered" (Heb. 5:8).

The Prophet Jeremiah's hope is for a renewed covenant with God, written not in stone but on believers' hearts. "I will put my law within them, and *I will write it on their hearts;* and I will be their God, and they shall be my people" (31:33).

All this would come about through God's initiative, as all past iniquities would be forgiven and forgotten. Thus, in the midst of brokenness and suffering, Jeremiah's words brought assurance of God's continued love and mercy.

As Jesus' hour—his Passion—draws near, he compares his death to a kernel of wheat that bears much fruit after falling into the earth and dying. As you anticipate Holy Week, what aspects of your own life need to die, or be transformed, in order for something new to spring forth?

Palm Sunday

I know Palm Sunday's exciting, but I also have a feeling it's going to get pretty dark over the next week, before it's time for Easter. Except—except that we're on God's time now. —Sara Miles.

Today's readings begin with the jubilant praise of the crowds as Jesus enters Jerusalem.

Jesus had sent two disciples ahead to procure a colt (Zech. 9:9). As he rode into the city, he was acclaimed with shouts of "Hosanna!" and longing for the kingdom of David (Mk. 11:9-10).

However, this moment of triumph ended quickly. Jesus' actions in Jerusalem, beginning with the cleansing of the temple the next day (vv. 15-18), would give the religious authorities new reasons to arrest and execute him (14:1).

But Jesus' suffering will have eternal purpose. Mark describes an unnamed woman who anoints Jesus with a costly ointment (14:3-9). Jesus responds to those who suggest wastefulness that "she has anointed my body beforehand for its burial." In contrast to the devotion of the woman, the disciple Judas plots with the chief priests to betray Jesus.

Mark presents Jesus' last meal with his disciples as a Passover that begins with Jesus predicting his betrayal. The bread and wine represent his body and blood, symbols of a new covenant. The meal concludes with another prediction of betrayal (vv. 26-31), this time by his closest followers, who will scatter like sheep (see Zech. 13:7) and deny him.

Jesus then proceeds to Gethsemane to pray. Jesus' deepest union with God occurs here. Although he is "distressed and agitated" as he asks "Abba, Father ... remove this cup from me"—he fully accepts the Father's will. He is accompanied by Peter, James, and John, though they cannot stay awake with him—another form of betrayal.

Jesus' arrest occurs as Judas kisses him—in a greeting that was normally a sign of respect and affection, but here becomes treachery. Now Jesus is totally alone, as he had predicted. He is taken before the high priest for questioning and charged with blasphemy—condemned to death for claiming to be the Messiah (v. 62).

In the meantime, Peter has followed to observe from a distance. As Jesus had predicted (v. 30), Peter denies three times that he knew Jesus.

The next morning Jesus is taken before the Roman Prefect Pontius Pilate (15:1-15). Pilate, not the Jewish court, had the legal authority to crucify Jesus. Pilate finds no fault with Jesus, and is initially reluctant to condemn him. He finally gives in to the demands of the crowd by releasing Barabbas and turning Jesus over for crucifixion.

Jesus is then beaten and mocked before being taken to Golgotha. Simon of Cyrene carries his cross (15:21), exemplifying what disciples *should* do. Darkness covers the land for three hours as Jesus is crucified between two other men (15:21-39). Jesus is taunted and asked why he doesn't save himself.

Then Jesus gives a loud cry and breathes his last. At that moment, the temple curtain is torn in half, and a Roman centurion exclaims that this man truly was God's Son (v. 39).

The third Servant Song of the Prophet Isaiah (50:4-9a) anticipates the rejection and suffering of the Messiah. The servant, by proclaiming God's word, has incurred insult and abuse. Nonetheless, he does not despair, knowing he can trust ultimately in the Lord.

Jesus, in *emptying himself of his Divine rights* to experience a criminal's death on a cross (Phil. 2:5-11), was fulfilling the Father's will that his ignominious death become a manifestation of *the glory of God*.

The Palm Sunday experience encompasses a wide range of emotions—from shouts of "Hosanna" when Jesus enters Jerusalem—to "Crucify him!" as he stands before Pilate. As Holy Week begins, imagine walking with Jesus through the events of the coming days. What is it like to accompany Christ on his journey to the cross?

Maundy Thursday

Jesus gives us His Body and His Blood in the liturgy no matter where that liturgy takes place: Calvary, a catacomb, a beach, a camp, a home, a simple chapel, or even a Cathedral. —Tom McGann.

On Maundy Thursday we are reminded of the transformative power of the Eucharist and of its connections to the Passover, which commemorates the escape of the Hebrews from slavery in Egypt.

After a series of plagues, the conflict between Moses and Pharaoh over the release of the Hebrews from Egypt reached a climax. Moses was assured by God that Pharaoh would allow them to leave after a final plague in which all the first-born of Egypt would die—including the offspring of the Pharaoh (Ex. 11:4-5).

Moses and Aaron gave each household instructions for slaughtering a year-old unblemished lamb at twilight. Blood from the lamb was to be painted on the doorposts as a sign that the Hebrews would be spared—passed over. They were to eat the lamb in haste and be ready to travel. This meal was to be observed each year throughout all generations as "a day of remembrance" of the Lord's redemption of Israel.

John's account of the Last Supper occurs on the eve of Passover and is not a Passover meal. Thus the crucifixion takes place on the day of preparation for Passover when the lambs were sacrificed (Jn. 19:31), pointing to Jesus as the true Paschal Lamb.

As the narrative begins, Jesus knows that his hour has come to leave this world and his beloved followers. Judas has already betrayed him. However, Jesus anticipated his union with the Father, from whom he had come and to whom he was returning (Jn. 13:3).

In humility, Jesus tied a towel around his waist, took a basin, and began to wash the feet of his disciples. It was customary to offer water to guests after a journey. But here the Lord acted as a slave, revealing the paradox of the Gospel in Jesus' extreme self-giving love.

Peter initially refused to allow Jesus to wash his feet. When Jesus responded that this was essential if he was to share in Jesus' life, Peter said: "Not my feet only but also my hands and my head!" Jesus replied that the symbolic washing of feet was enough. The true cleansing Jesus brings is *forgiveness of sins* through his death. And this is offered to all, even to the one who would betray him (v. 11).

Jesus explains to his disciples that soon the Father will be glorified by the Son. Calling his disciples "little children," Jesus tells them they cannot come where he is going, and offers a new commandment: "Just as I have loved you, you also should love one another" (v. 34).

In Paul's account in 1 Corinthians there was disagreement over proper observance of the Lord's Supper (1 Cor. 11:17-22). Paul declared that he handed on to his converts what he had received from the Lord. On the night Jesus was betrayed, he took bread, gave thanks, and broke it to share with the others. He identifies the broken bread with his own body about to be offered on the cross: "This is my body that is for you" (v. 24).

The cup of blessing he equates with his blood that he would soon shed. "This cup is the new covenant in my blood" (v. 25). Just as Moses sealed God's covenant with blood (Ex. 24:8), the blood of Christ is taken in remembrance of him, proclaiming the Lord's saving death until he shall return again.

On the night before he died, Jesus shared a final meal with his disciples. In the future, they were to partake of the bread and wine in remembrance of him. In what ways do you experience the presence of Christ in the Eucharist?

Good Friday

Only by facing our mortality can we come in touch with the life that transcends death. Our imperfections open for us the vision of the perfect life that God in and through Jesus has promised us. —Henri Nouwen.

On Good Friday it is customary to read the Passion from the Gospel of John. Jesus' "hour" (Jn. 13:1) has finally come, as he glorifies God and is victorious over his adversaries.

After the Last Supper, Jesus and his disciples go to a garden near the Kidron Valley, where Jesus is arrested (18:1-11). Jesus steps forward and tells the men that he is the one they seek; there is no need for Judas to betray him with a kiss. Jesus rebukes Peter for slicing off a slave's ear with his sword.

Jesus is first questioned by Annas, the father-in-law of the high priest Caiaphas. Here Peter denies the Lord three times, just as Jesus had predicted (vv. 15-18, 25-27).

In the early morning hours, Jesus is bound over to Pilate, the Roman governor of Palestine. When asked by Pilate if he is a king, he says, "My kingdom is not from this world" (v. 36). Though Pilate cannot find a case against Jesus, the crowd calls for the release of the bandit Barabbas.

Pilate has Jesus flogged, and the soldiers mock him by dressing him in purple with a crown of thorns. The local religious leaders insist that Jesus should die for claiming to be the Son of God (19:7).

When asked if he realizes that Pilate has the authority to decide whether he lives or dies, Jesus responds that the only power Pilate holds over him is that conferred by God (v. 11). After the chief priests declare their loyalty to the Roman emperor, Pilate hands Jesus over for crucifixion. According to Roman custom, the charge against a condemned criminal was to be fixed above him on the cross. Thus Pilate had the words inscribed: "Jesus of Nazareth, the King of the Jews," and refused to modify it to "This man said, I am King of the Jews" (v. 21).

In John's Gospel, Jesus speaks three times from the cross. Among those who watched were four women, including Jesus' mother and the unidentified beloved disciple. We see the depth and intensity of Jesus' love as he entrusts Mary and the disciple to each other's care.

Knowing that all is now completed, Jesus speaks once again in fulfillment of the Scriptures (see Ps. 69:21): "I am thirsty." He is then given wine on a hyssop branch. This is a reminder of the Passover preparations, when the blood of a lamb was applied on doorposts with a hyssop branch (Ex. 12:22-23).

Jesus now utters his final words: "It is finished" (19:30). He then bows his head and gives up his spirit. With his mission fully accomplished, his pronouncement becomes a declaration of victory.

Hebrews expresses the completeness of Christ's sacrifice. Jesus came to do God's will in an offering that would take away sin once and for all. There is now to be a new covenant written on the hearts and minds of God's people. The blood of Jesus has opened a way into the eternal presence and brought new life to the world.

The assurance of God's presence in the midst of suffering is reflected in the Prophet Isaiah's description of the marred appearance of the Suffering Servant who is rejected by the world (52:13–53:12). Nevertheless, he will be vindicated by God. Although despised and held of no account, he is proclaimed to have borne the sins of many, and brought light and life to the world.

As the most solemn day in the Church Year, Good Friday is "good" because of eternal life brought about through Christ's victory on the cross. How are our lives transformed as we share in the suffering of Christ?

EASTER

Our peering into the empty tomb forever changes us. How inexhaustibly rich the Easter event is! … What better way to celebrate the feast of Easter: to dance for sheer joy! —Wendy Wright.

Easter is the principal feast of the Christian year. Celebrated as the "Great Fifty Days," the Easter season begins on Easter Day and concludes fifty days later on the Day of Pentecost. On the fortieth day, we commemorate the Ascension of Jesus as a glorious return to heaven.

The readings for the Easter season focus on the transforming power of the Resurrection and follow a similar pattern in all three years of the Lectionary cycle. Easter Day offers a choice of Gospel readings: John's story may be read in all three years; or in Year B, Mark's account is an option. On the Second Sunday we always read the Resurrection story featuring Thomas in the Gospel of John. The Third Sunday is the Resurrection appearance of Jesus on the road to Emmaus, found in Luke. Easter 4 is "Good Shepherd Sunday," with the Gospel taken from John 10 in which Jesus proclaims, "I am the good shepherd." The Gospel readings for Easter 5, 6, and 7 are from Jesus' farewell discourse in John. As the Easter season comes to an end, we celebrate the coming of the promised Holy Spirit on the Day of Pentecost with the dramatic story from Acts 2.

During the Easter season, the first Lesson on each Sunday is from the Book of Acts, which records the witness of the early Church to the life, death, and Resurrection of Jesus. The Epistles in Year B are from the First Letter of John, drawing on themes from the Gospel of John.

At the heart of Christian faith—as the glorious manifestation of God's love—the Resurrection empowers those who put their trust in the Risen Lord. Christ has overcome death and brought the promise of everlasting life to the world.

"Alleluia, Christ is risen! The Lord is risen indeed!"

Easter Day

Easter Sunday is the most important Sunday. It is the Sunday of all Sundays. It is the day of the new beginning of the entire cosmos, the day of resurrection.   —Robert E. Webber.

All the Gospel accounts of Easter morning include the fact of the women being first at the empty tomb. Although there are differences, Mary Magdalene plays a significant role in all the tellings.

In John's version, Mary Magdalene went alone to the tomb in the early morning. When she saw the entrance stone rolled away and the tomb empty, she assumed the body had been stolen and ran to tell the other disciples. At her announcement, Peter and the unidentified beloved disciple ran to the tomb.

Both men observed the linen cloths and the folded head wrapping. The beloved disciple "saw and believed." Yet he did not comprehend Jesus' Resurrection (20:9). When the disciples returned to their homes, Mary remained weeping outside the tomb. Two angels robed in white asked her why she was weeping. "They have taken away my Lord, and I do not know where they have laid him" (v. 13).

Hearing a voice, Mary turned as another figure inquired why she was weeping. Mary assumed he was the overseer, and asked where the body of her Lord had been taken. Only when Jesus called her by name did Mary recognize him and respond *"Rabbouni!"* She reached to embrace Jesus, but he restrained her, "because I have not yet ascended to the Father" (v. 17a).

Mary returned to the disciples as the first witness of the Resurrected Lord. The heart of the Easter revelation is her astounding message: *"I have seen the Lord."*

In Mark's account, Mary Magdalene and three other women come to the tomb. They are greeted by a young man in white who tells them that Jesus of Nazareth, who was crucified, is not there: *"He has been raised"* (16:6). They are to tell the disciples and Peter what they have seen.

But instead, the women flee, afraid to tell anyone. The experience was too wonderful, too fearsome for them to enter into all at once.

During the Easter season, the first Lesson is from Acts. Here Peter explains the Gospel to Gentiles in the home of the Roman centurion Cornelius. Peter had realized through a dream (Acts 10:9-16) that *God's salvation was for everyone.* This message of peace was sent to the world through Jesus Christ, Lord of all (v. 36).

Empowered by the Holy Spirit, Jesus went about doing good and healing. However, some were threatened by him and crucified him. But God raised him from the dead on the third day, after which he appeared bodily to close disciples.

Those who saw the Risen Christ are now called to testify that Jesus, foretold by the prophets and ordained by God to forgive sins, is "judge of the living and the dead" (v. 42).

In 1 Corinthians 15, Paul affirms that Jesus died for our sins, was buried, and on the third day was raised from the dead. The truth of the Resurrection is attested by eyewitnesses—and last of all to Paul himself, whose own calling derived from an experience of the Risen Lord.

The Resurrection is the keystone of God's plan to restore humanity and all creation. Now a radical new way of viewing the world is possible, as we share in the promise of eternal life.

The Easter celebration is the central event of our Christian faith. How does the world—and especially your own life—continue to be transformed by the miracle of the Resurrection?

Easter 2

Christ's love breaks through every rolled stone, bolted door, solid wall; every closed and locked heart; so that no one is left out. Touch me, the risen Christ says. Draw close to me. Let all the world come to me. —K. Jeanne Person.

We declare to you what we have seen and heard ... (1 Jn. 1:1). Jesus, as the "word of life," has existed from all eternity. We have fellowship with God as our Father and with Jesus Christ the Son, and can rejoice to live in the light.

As today's passage in John 20 begins, the disciples are gathered on the evening of Easter Day. Since Jesus had been condemned on charges of sedition, his followers are meeting behind locked doors, fearful of the Jewish authorities.

Earlier in the day, Peter and the beloved disciple had witnessed the empty tomb; and Mary Magdalene had told the disciples: "I have seen the Lord." However, none of them were ready to believe Mary's report.

Jesus suddenly appeared before them. His unexpected presence in the locked room verified his resurrection in a physical body. Yet it is also a spiritual body (see 1 Cor. 15:35-55), as Jesus is able to pass through locked doors or vanish from sight. His appearance seems continuous with his earthly existence, bearing the marks of his Passion. He is not a phantom, but their Lord in a recognizable, imperishable body.

As Jesus enters the room, he greets them: "Peace be with you"—and his words calm their troubled hearts in a way the world cannot (see Jn. 14:27). These words also express forgiveness toward the followers who had abandoned him at the cross.

When Jesus shows the disciples the marks on his hands and side, they rejoice. Mary's message is now confirmed by their own experience.

Once again he speaks of peace, and then entrusts them with a mission: "As the Father has sent me, so I send you." As the Son has revealed the Father, now they are to reveal the Son to the world.

However, they cannot accomplish this on their own. So the Lord breathes on them—just as in the beginning God had breathed life into Adam (Gen. 2:7). *"Receive the Holy Spirit."* This infuses them to be witnesses to Jesus' saving power. Even the ministry of "binding and loosing" from sin is now to be carried on by the Apostles, continuing Christ's mission.

The second Resurrection appearance to the gathered disciples occurs a week later. The Apostle Thomas had previously been absent. When told of the Lord's appearance, he had stated the need to see Jesus' wounds for himself. When Jesus appears again, he offers Thomas the proof he sought: "Do not doubt but believe" (v. 27).

Thomas' disbelief is immediately transformed into a profound statement of faith as he exalts the Risen Jesus: "My Lord and my God!"—going far beyond the response of the other disciples. Jesus then proclaims blessing on those who have come to true faith without the need for sight.

The Resurrection of Jesus brought about a new understanding of human relationships and life in community. Today's reading from Acts (4:32-35) describes the believers' commitment to live in mutual generosity and compassion, as witnesses to God's love. They held all things in common and continued to testify to the Resurrection of Jesus.

At the appearance of the Risen Lord, Thomas exalts Jesus as "My Lord and my God." How have you come to know Jesus as Lord in your life? How do you share this belief with others?

Easter 3

The Resurrection means creation healed. When submitted to the God of Easter, all of life's scarring events can be transfigured. —H. King Oehmig.

Jesus was indeed *alive* and *present* more powerfully than ever, appearing at unexpected times and places. Yet this was difficult to grasp, and everyone struggled to comprehend this miraculous event.

Earlier the disciples had received as "an idle tale" the astounding news from Mary Magdalene that Jesus had been raised from the dead (Lk. 24:1-12). Later in the day the witness of the women was confirmed by two who walked to Emmaus with Jesus and ate with him (vv. 13-35). After Jesus left them, they set out for Jerusalem to share their experience with the disciples.

However, those who had not seen were still confused, continuing to question those who *had* seen. As the disciples discussed the day's momentous events, Jesus suddenly appeared among them with the familiar greeting, "Peace be with you." They were terrified, taking him for a ghost. To calm their initial fears and prove he was indeed flesh and bones, he invited them to touch his hands and feet—to see that his Risen body was no less substantial than their own.

As further verification of his physical reality, Jesus asked for a piece of broiled fish and ate it before them. Through this simple act, the Easter miracle was revealed in the most human way: eating with friends. Jesus' Resurrected body had been raised into the new life of the age to come. Death is overcome "when this perishable body puts on imperishability, and this mortal body puts on immortality ... " (1 Cor. 15:54).

As in the conversation on the road to Emmaus (Lk. 24:27, 32), here also Jesus "opened their minds to understand the scriptures" (v. 45), how Moses and the prophets foretold that *God's Messiah had to suffer and die* before he could be raised.

Easter is the event through which Scripture is to be interpreted, and the Resurrection must now be proclaimed to the world. Once Jesus has explained that his ministry fulfills God's promises through the Cross and Resurrection, he commissions the disciples as *witnesses to God's action in Christ*. They now have the power and duty to proclaim repentance and forgiveness to all—beginning in Jerusalem.

This was the good news that the disciples were to preach to the nations; but they were to stay in Jerusalem until they received the Father's promise and were "clothed with power from on high" (Lk. 24:49) through the Holy Spirit (Acts 2:1-4).

In today's reading from Acts, Peter addresses a crowd after he and John had healed a man born lame (3:1-10). Peter explains to the amazed listeners that this miracle has come through the power of the Risen Lord (v. 16). He explains that Jesus is the fulfillment of God's saving purpose for humanity.

The writer of 1 John emphasizes that being a follower of the Risen Lord includes living in a manner that reflects the actions of Jesus himself. Through the love of God we are claimed as God's children. But we find ourselves separated from the world that refuses to acknowledge God. Our share in bringing about the Lord's purposes is to *continue to seek the righteousness* that we see modeled most perfectly in Christ Jesus. "Everyone who does what is right is righteous, just as he is righteous" (1 Jn. 3:7).

Throughout the Easter season we focus on the implications of the transforming power of the Resurrection. What are you called to do in your daily life in response to the Resurrection of Jesus?

Easter 4

Great Shepherd of the sheep, we are your flock, and we bring to you gifts and offerings from our hearts and lives. Be our Shepherd always, and send us forth, that we might bring to other sheep the message of your love. Amen.   —Thomas L. Weitzel.

Scripture is full of references to shepherds and shepherding, especially the comforting words of Psalm 23: "The Lord is my Shepherd." We find this image also in the words of the Prophet Ezekiel, who promised that God would raise up a true shepherd for the people (34:23-24). John's Gospel saw this vocation fulfilled in Jesus, who proclaims: "I am the good shepherd" (Jn. 10:11).

Ezekiel depicts the leaders of the nation as false, unworthy shepherds, in contrast to the Lord's care for the flock (Ezek. 34:1-16). Jesus considers the sheep's welfare before his own safety; while his opponents are like self-serving hired hands.

Any true shepherd cares about the sheep. But there is only one shepherd—Jesus—who willingly offers his life for the flock (Jn. 10:11, 15, 17, 18), granting eternal life and ending the reign of death forever. Jesus knows the sheep, as they know him, loving them with the same love the Father has for him. *Laying down his life* is the Gospel's way of describing Jesus' redeeming sacrifice (see Jn. 10:30). Jesus has come to earth to do God's will and to reveal the Father's love.

But the flock is not limited to a few disciples in Galilee and Judea. Other sheep who "do not belong to this fold" (v. 16a) also must be included. Jesus intends that all the sheep will hear his voice and follow him. Thus "there will be one flock, one shepherd" (v. 16c).

As this message goes forth from Jerusalem, the voice of the Lord will be heard through the words of those who make up his "body." In this vision of God's Kingdom on earth, there will be no separation due to race, culture, or social status.

And just as Jesus lays down his life willingly, he also has the power to take it up again (v. 18) *through the Resurrection*—revealing God's love for the world. Thus on this Good Shepherd Sunday, we can trust in the salvation that flows from the Risen Christ.

The author of 1 John echoes the words of the Evangelist by writing that *as recipients of Christ's redeeming sacrifice* we, like the Good Shepherd, ought to "lay down our lives for one another" (3:16). However, this love is not just sentiment, but concrete actions for the welfare of others: " ... let us love, not in word or speech, but in truth and action" (v. 18). In our love for Christ and obedience to his commandments, we are assured of God's abiding presence through the Holy Spirit (v. 24b).

In Acts, the transforming power of the Resurrection can be seen in the actions of the Apostles. Those who had once hid in fear now boldly proclaim the power of the Risen Lord, despite opposition from the authorities.

Peter and John healed a man born lame by commanding him to walk in the name of Jesus Christ of Nazareth. As they announced the power of Jesus to the crowd, Peter and John were arrested and taken into custody (Acts 3:1-10; 4:1-3).

On the following day, the religious authorities of Jerusalem questioned Peter and John and asked by whose power they were able to perform this healing. "Filled with the Holy Spirit" (4:8), Peter testified that this saving restoration is found only in the Risen Lord.

What does it mean for you when Jesus proclaims, "I am the good shepherd"? How is the Risen Lord the shepherd of your life? How are you called to live your life as you follow Jesus as your shepherd?

Easter 5

Our existence, our life, our thought—all of this comes from the Logos, and apart from Him, we can bear no fruit. —Robert Emmet Barron.

I am the true vine, and my Father is the vinegrower (Jn. 15:1).

The hardy vine was found everywhere in Palestine and was a metaphor for Israel in the Old Testament (Ezek. 19:10-14). The Prophet Jeremiah used the image of a vine that had grown wild to illustrate how Israel had failed to fulfill God's purposes for planting and nurturing it (Jer. 2:21).

When Jesus proclaims, "I am the true vine," he affirms that he embodies what Israel was called to be. In Christ, *Israel's destiny is completed.* Jesus is the source of life for the disciples. And God the Father is the planter. All vines need to be carefully tended by a gardener, with dead wood cut away in order for them to produce useful fruit.

Because the disciples have accepted the word of Jesus, they have already been cleansed (Jn. 15:3), or pruned, and are therefore fruitful "branches." The branch that is nourished by the central vine, Jesus, will bear much fruit; but one that loses that connection cannot. *Mutual indwelling* is the way of life and productivity for the disciples. Thus Jesus calls them to "Abide in me as I abide in you."

With Christ, we have the power to do the work God calls us to; but apart from Christ, we can do nothing. And what the community asks in Jesus' name will be supplied by God (v. 7). Indeed, for branches abiding in total union with Christ, nothing will be impossible.

In today's Epistle, the mutual nature of God's love is revealed through Jesus, who laid down his life for us. Just as *God loves us,* we are to *love one another.* In truth, one who does not love a fellow disciple whom he *has* seen cannot truly know and love God whom he *has not* seen. "God is love" (1 Jn. 4:16); we abide in God and God in us.

The conversion of the Ethiopian man in Acts 8 shows the Church growing beyond the religious, cultural, and geographical bounds of Israel through the Holy Spirit, as foretold by Jesus (Acts 1:8). As the passage begins, an angel of the Lord has sent the Apostle Philip from Samaria down the wilderness road between Jerusalem and Gaza.

When Philip encounters a fellow traveler, the Spirit leads him to approach the man's chariot. We learn that he is a eunuch and a high court official in charge of the entire treasury of the queen of Ethiopia, who was returning from Jerusalem. This man, as both a Gentile and a eunuch, would have been considered an outsider.

As Philip runs alongside the man's chariot, he hears him reading from the Prophet Isaiah. Philip gets into the chariot, and the man asks him to explain the passage, from one of the Servant Songs of Isaiah (53:7-8). Christian tradition had already identified the crucified Jesus as the fulfillment of this prophetic oracle. Thus Philip proclaims "the good news about Jesus" (Acts 8:35) in a manner reminiscent of the post-Resurrection Lord opening minds to understand the Scriptures (see Lk. 24:45).

The Ethiopian man eagerly accepts the Gospel and asks to be baptized. After Philip baptized him, "the Spirit of the Lord snatched Philip away" (v. 39) to Azotus, north of Gaza. There he continued preaching the Gospel all the way to Caesarea. The Ethiopian man "went on his way rejoicing" in response to his newfound faith.

As you reflect on the image of Jesus as the true vine, how does it define our relationship with Jesus? What aspects of your life need to be nurtured or pruned in order for you to bear good fruit—to abide in Jesus as he abides in us?

Easter 6

Love for God does not consist of ecstatic experiences or private feelings, but of concrete, public, and visible obedience: by confessing faith in God's Son, and by loving God's other children. —Brian Peterson.

The Gospel passage is a continuation of last week's reading (Jn. 15:1-8) from Jesus' farewell discourse to his disciples on the night before he died. Jesus declares, "As the Father has loved me, so I have loved you; abide in my love" (Jn. 15:9). Just as Jesus has been faithful in keeping the Father's commandments, his followers are to do likewise, so that their "joy may be complete" (v. 11).

"This is my commandment, that you love one another as I have loved you" (v. 12). This love is expressed by actions, not just words or feelings, and is seen most clearly in the way of self-sacrifice—in laying down one's life for one's friends, as Jesus did for us.

When the disciples obey Jesus' commandments and share his love, they are no longer "servants"—they are his friends (vv. 14-15). This friendship is a manifestation of Jesus' steadfast love and a call to service and faithfulness.

John's Gospel makes no stronger statement on the call to vocation than here: Disciples are chosen to bear fruit that should last (v. 16) as they carry on Jesus' mission. To this Jesus adds a promise: When a disciple's will is in conformity with God's will, which is *love,* there is no limit to what God can and will do in that person's life.

We have not chosen Jesus; he has chosen us. We may never understand the reasons—it is enough to love one another and glorify the Father's name by keeping the commandments given to us. "I am giving you these commands so that you may love one another" (v. 17).

This truth is echoed in today's Epistle, where we read that we are children of God by loving and obeying God's commandments: "For the love of God is this, that we obey his commandments" (1 Jn. 5:3a). However, the commandments are not burdens to be borne, but are the way to life and fulfillment. "And this is the victory that conquers the world, our faith" (v. 4b).

The Acts of the Apostles gives further witness to the power of the Spirit, as *the love of God through Christ* is extended to all. Today's passage is the conclusion of Peter's visit to the household of the Roman centurion Cornelius, the first Gentile convert as recorded in Acts (10:1-48).

Previously, Peter had a dream in which he was commanded to eat food considered to be unclean. When he refused, a voice declared, "What God has made clean, you must not call profane" (v. 15).

Peter, emboldened by his new insight that God accepts anyone who fears the Lord and does what is right (10:35), traveled to the home of Cornelius. As Peter proclaimed the Gospel message to Cornelius' household, the Holy Spirit came upon them all—even the Gentiles—and they began speaking in tongues and praising God in a scene reminiscent of the Day of Pentecost (Acts 2:4). The Jews who had accompanied Peter were astounded that the Spirit should be given to Gentiles, even as Peter ordered that they were to be baptized in the name of Jesus.

This is in essence *a Gentile Pentecost*. The gifts of the Holy Spirit and baptism are now extended to all who hear and accept the love of God through Christ. This is indeed a "marvelous thing."

Jesus gives us the command to love one another as he loves us. What are the characteristics of this love? How can we receive and demonstrate this abiding love in our daily lives?

Ascension Day

Be Thou exalted above the heavens, O God! We have not seen it, but we believe. —St. Augustine of Hippo.

The Ascension of Jesus into heaven, commemorated forty days after Easter, is the climax of his earthly ministry. At this point of transition from the Resurrection to Pentecost, we are living in an interim state between promise and fulfillment.

Jesus, in his final Resurrection appearance at the end of Luke, reminded his disciples that *everything written about him had been fulfilled* (Lk. 24:45-47). His suffering, death, and Resurrection were a part of God's plan of salvation. The disciples had been witnesses to these events; now they were to proclaim redemption to all the world.

Jesus tells them to remain in Jerusalem until they are "clothed with power from on high" (v. 49)—as Mary was told at the Annunciation: "The Holy Spirit will come upon you, and the power of the Most High will overshadow you" (Lk. 1:35).

In former times, Joshua had been filled with the Spirit of wisdom from Moses (Dt. 34:9); and Elisha had received a double portion of Elijah's spirit upon his departure (2 Ki. 2:9, 15). Now the power of the Holy Spirit that had infused Jesus' ministry would be bestowed on his followers as they carried on his work and declared openly what they had once held in silence. The spirit of Jesus will now be available to followers in all times and places as *Emmanuel—God with us* (Mt. 1:24).

Jesus led the disciples to Bethany, where he blessed them and "was carried up into heaven" (Lk. 24:51). The disciples responded with great joy, as they worshiped him and returned to Jerusalem, just as Jesus had instructed. There they praised God in the temple as they awaited the coming empowerment of the Spirit.

In Acts 1 we read that after the Resurrection, Jesus appeared to his followers over forty days, preaching the Kingdom of God and commanding them to wait in Jerusalem for the "promise of the Father": the gift of a new baptism with the Holy Spirit (v. 5).

When the disciples ask him whether or not this will occur when God restores the Kingdom to Israel, Jesus explains that they have no need to know the times of what the Father does. God's purposes go far beyond the temporal restoration of Israel to enable a proclamation of the Gospel that is broad and inclusive.

The disciples will receive power when the Holy Spirit comes to them, equipping them as witnesses for Christ even "to the ends of the earth" (v. 8).

When Jesus had given them this assurance, he was "lifted up, and a cloud took him out of their sight" (v. 9). Then, as the disciples stood gazing up into the sky, two men in white robes appeared, asking "Why do you stand looking up toward heaven?" This Jesus would return, they affirmed, "in the same way as you saw him go" (v. 11b).

In Ephesians we read how God put the Divine power to work in Christ by raising him from the dead and *seating him at God's right hand in the heavenly places* (1:20). Included is a prayer for spiritual wisdom and revelation, so that, with the eyes of their hearts enlightened (v. 18), believers might realize their rich and glorious inheritance.

God's power, as manifested in the Resurrection of Christ, exceeds that of all other temporal and eternal authorities, now and in the future. Christ has been made head over all for the sake of the Church his Body.

As Jesus ascended into heaven, he bestowed his mission on his disciples. How does Jesus continue to be present as we carry on his work in the world today?

Easter 7

Christ will come again. We await his coming in glory. There needs to be a shift in our thinking as we close Eastertide and move toward Ordinary Time: how do we inhabit and occupy the already but not yet? —Porter Taylor.

Jesus' High Priestly Prayer (Jn. 17:1-26) was offered on behalf of his closest disciples on the night before his death. In it Jesus prays for the protection and unity of his followers in a hostile world after he is no longer with them.

During his earthly ministry, Jesus watched over the community God had entrusted to him, and no disciples came to harm except Judas. But now that Jesus will no longer be present physically, he prays for the Father to protect them. He asks *that they be one,* even as Jesus and the Father are one (v. 11b).

As he is returning to his Father, Jesus recounts the joy he has known in constant awareness of God's presence. The message that Jesus has brought to the world, only to face rejection, he gives to his followers. Because he loves the unredeemed world just as his Father does, it is now the disciples' mission and identity as well. And since it derives from Jesus, and not the world, enmity from the world is inevitable (v. 14).

God, who has been with Jesus, will now also preserve the disciples from evil. "I am not asking you to take them out of the world, but I ask you to protect them from the evil one" (v. 15).

Jesus goes on to pray that they may be made holy through the truth of the Father's message (v. 17)—and then carry it out into the world as Jesus did. By his own sacrifice he is consecrating—"sanctifying"—himself, even as he is about to face arrest.

Christ's self-revelation to his disciples is now complete. Even though they will fail badly in the next few hours as Jesus is arrested, the Gospel witness will survive. Jesus' prayer is an ongoing intercession that they be *made holy* by the truth that they have received from him and to which they bear witness.

The disciples for whom Jesus prayed are our representatives; thus, as the Lord prayed for and sent *them,* so he prays for and sends *us* today as well.

The reading from Acts 1:15-17, 21-26 illustrates the Apostolic foundation of the community that Christ called into being, as a new Apostle is selected to replace Judas, the betrayer. Jesus had chosen twelve individuals to be his Apostles—an inner circle who received his teachings in order to continue his work. With the loss of Judas, the number of Apostles was reduced to eleven; and it was deemed important that the number twelve, recalling the twelve tribes of Israel, be maintained.

Anyone considered had to have accompanied Jesus from the beginning of his ministry at the Baptism by John to his Ascension, and thus have been a witness to the Resurrection. This meant that two faithful men were eligible: Joseph called Barsabbas and Matthias. As those assembled prayed to the Lord, the lot fell on Matthias. Now the number of Apostles was complete, and the community was prepared to receive the empowering of the Spirit and carry on the mission entrusted to them by Jesus.

The Epistle today makes clear that this new community is called to believe and to proclaim that *Jesus is the Son of God.* Through Jesus, God gives us eternal life; and without him there is only death. "Whoever has the Son has life; whoever does not have the Son of God does not have life" (1 Jn. 5:12). Today we are offered a challenge to understand and live out this empowerment.

On the night before he died, Jesus offered a prayer for his disciples. How does this prayer continue to strengthen and encourage us today?

Day of Pentecost

Bethlehem was God with us, Calvary was God for us, and Pentecost is God in us. —**Robert Baer.**

At his Ascension, Jesus promised his disciples that they would *receive power when the Holy Spirit has come upon you ...*

Pentecost is Greek for *fiftieth,* and in Israel, the first spring crops were harvested fifty days after planting. However, by the time of Jesus, the festival held on this day was often a commemoration of the giving of Torah at Sinai. But for the Christian community, Pentecost would become a celebration of the *new life of the Church* through God's gift of the Holy Spirit.

Previously, John the Baptist had proclaimed that Jesus came to baptize with the Holy Spirit and fire. Thus, on the Day of Pentecost, God's Spirit filled the house where the disciples were staying with a "sound like the rush of a violent wind" (Acts 2:2). In addition, divided tongues as of fire came to rest on *each of them.* No one was left without a share of God's empowering gift.

Filled with the Holy Spirit, the disciples burst into praise and spoke in languages they did not know, "as the Spirit gave them ability" (Acts 2:4). Miraculously, these words were recognized by people who had come from many different nations. What they heard was a recounting of "God's deeds of power" (v. 11). In this "reversal" of the story of the Tower of Babel (Gen. 11:1-9), we see a foreshadowing of the universal mission of the Church.

But there were some who disbelieved and accused them of being drunk. Thus Peter reminded them of the words from Joel: " ... I will pour out my Spirit upon all flesh, and your sons and your daughters shall prophesy" (2:17a). This powerful effect became a reality as three thousand were converted on that day (v. 41).

The Gospel passage tells how Jesus, on the night before he was crucified, assured his disciples that after he left, the Father would send an Advocate, the Spirit of truth, to be with them. The truths that the

Father had given to Jesus would now be the message the disciples themselves would carry forth.

Jesus acknowledges the disciples' sorrow and confusion as he tells them that he must leave them. Yet his departure is necessary. If he were to remain, it would not be possible for the Holy Spirit to come to them (Jn. 16:7).

The work of this Advocate will be to "prove the world wrong about sin and righteousness and judgment" (v. 8). The apparent victory of the "ruler of this world" (v. 11) in bringing about the death of Jesus will be *reversed* when Jesus returns and is glorified by the Father.

As Jesus' earthly experience with his disciples is coming to an end, he has much more he wishes to share with them. But they are not yet able to comprehend God's complete revelation in Jesus. Thus the Spirit will guide the disciples into this truth, and *will be continually present* to enable them to hold onto it and give glory to God. The Spirit also calls *us* to serve as witnesses to Jesus in our world today.

Paul, in his letter to the Romans, likens this work of the Spirit in bringing about a new creation to the pangs of childbirth, as the world hopes for and anticipates the painful transformation or "birth" that is about to take place (8:24-25).

When we do not know how to pray, the Spirit helps us in our struggles and "intercedes with sighs too deep for words" (v. 26), bringing us into accord with the will of God.

As you reflect on the dramatic coming of the Holy Spirit, how do you recognize the presence of the Spirit in your own life, in the Church, and in the world?

ORDINARY TIME – THE SEASON AFTER PENTECOST

Ordinary time is not supposed to be viewed as "ordinary" in the sense of lacking meaning or being a "break" from the Liturgical Year. The opposite is actually true: Ordinary Time celebrates "the mystery of Christ" in *all* its aspects. —David Bennett.

The Season After Pentecost or Ordinary Time begins with Trinity Sunday—the only time in the Church Year when we commemorate a doctrine of the Church; and ends with the Reign of Christ or Christ the King Sunday, just before Advent begins. The season is "ordinary" in that no particular special events in the life of Jesus are commemorated. This is the longest season of the Church Year, with twenty-three or twenty-eight Sundays, depending on the date of Easter Day.

In accordance with the Gospel focus of Year B, the Gospel readings for this season are semi-continuous passages from Mark, with the exception of Propers 12-16, which are taken from the "Bread of Life" discourse in John 6. The Old Testament readings take us through the stories of David in Samuel and Kings, before shifting to passages from the Wisdom books: the Song of Solomon, Proverbs, and Job, along with Esther and Ruth. The Epistles include readings from 2 Corinthians, followed by Ephesians, James, and Hebrews. The only exceptions to these patterns are found on All Saints' Day and the final Sunday of the year.

In Ordinary Time we experience the fullness of the biblical story from Sunday to Sunday. We follow in the footsteps of Jesus in the Gospels as he preaches, teaches, and heals. The Old Testament passages remind us of the history of God's people. The authors of the Epistles reflect on life in the early Church community and the ways we are called to live in relationship with God and one another.

This is a season for growth as the Church; and we as individuals are challenged to live out our calling in the world of *fulfilling the mission of God in Christ*.

Trinity Sunday

Like Nicodemus, know that we are spirit with the One Spirit, and we know that we have not only been born anew in this Spirit but adopted as children and heirs of the eternal Father, brothers and sisters of the eternal Son. —Katherine Merrell Glen.

The doctrine of the Trinity comes down to us from both the biblical witness and Christian experience. Although this doctrine is not explicitly formulated in Scripture, today's passages are examples of the spiritual roots of the Trinity.

Human speech is inadequate to describe the manifold aspects of our infinite God. But one of the ways we get a glimpse of the glory and majesty of the Divine is through the visions of prophets and mystics, as in the call of Isaiah.

Isaiah's vision unites heaven and earth, as he describes the heavenly court where the Lord is enthroned in a vast temple attended by six-winged seraphs singing "Holy, holy, holy ... " (6: 3). This anticipates praise of God as Father, Son, and Holy Spirit.

This passage reflects awe and wonder at the glory of God, as well as the transforming power of God's presence. We learn that prophetic speech is not derived from human intelligence, but is a gift—indeed a mandate—from God.

In the Gospel, Nicodemus, a truth-seeking religious leader, addresses Jesus as "Rabbi"—one learned in Torah. Further signifying his respect, Nicodemus recognizes the signs that indicate Jesus has come from God.

Jesus proceeds to tell Nicodemus what is most necessary for salvation: "No one can see the kingdom of God without being born from above" (Jn. 3:3). This is an inner transformation, a reorientation of the self *from the world* and directly *toward God*.

However, Nicodemus cannot move beyond a literal understanding of Jesus' words. The rebirth of which Jesus speaks is a *spiritual* rather than a physical birth.

Jesus continues, saying "no one can enter the kingdom of God without being born of water and Spirit" (v. 5). Birth from above is a *gift of faith* that enables one to believe. "What is born of the flesh is flesh, and what is born of the Spirit is spirit" (v. 6). Like the wind, God's Spirit cannot be predicted or fit into human categories.

But Nicodemus, still thinking literally, remains confused. Jesus can speak of "heavenly things" (v. 12) because, as the Son of Man—the link between heaven and earth—he is the one who has "descended from heaven" to bring redemption.

The familiar words of verse 16 reveal the way to eternal life for *those who believe in Jesus' name.* The Son comes not to condemn the world, but *to offer salvation* to all.

Thus through this dialogue with Nicodemus we learn that *God, as Father,* offers us boundless love. *God the Son* is the Incarnate one through whom we have eternal life. And *God the Holy Spirit* infuses our lives in mysterious and surprising ways.

The Apostle Paul offers us the image of God as our adoptive parent. We are flesh, but God is Spirit. We may live out our lives wholly in terms of the physical; but if we do, the consequence is death (Rom. 8:13). However, if we are led by the Spirit of God, *we will live.* God has given us the Holy Spirit, and through adoption we become God's children, shaped by the values of God's Kingdom.

By being present with us, the Spirit enables us to know and to call on God as *Abba,* our Father, just as Christ did.

Trinity Sunday is the only time in the Church Year when we commemorate a doctrine of the Church, as we attempt to understand the manifold aspects of the Divine. How do you experience God as Father (Creator), Son (Redeemer), and Holy Spirit (Sanctifier)? How does the mystery and revelation of a Triune God shape your spiritual life?

Proper 1 Year B See Epiphany 6

Proper 2 Year B See Epiphany 7

Proper 3 Year B See Epiphany 8

Proper 4

The gospels are full of stories where Jesus ignores the boundaries imposed by acceptable religious and social practice, and openly disregards man-made laws and regulations in order to show compassion. He consistently lets sinners and outcasts know that they are wanted and loved by God, even if they are despised by everyone else. —David Vryhof, SSJE.

For the Hebrews, the Sabbath Day was to remain free from work and commercial trade. Indeed, Sabbath-keeping was a significant mark of Jewish distinctiveness. In Jesus' time, these regulations had become increasingly demanding.

Jesus did not question this or reject these inherited laws, but rather *brought them to fulfillment.* When they strengthened the covenant community, Jesus encouraged them. However, when these same laws intruded on relations with God and neighbor, Jesus denounced them.

In the first incident in today's Gospel (Mk. 2:23-28), the Pharisees challenge Jesus for allowing his disciples to pluck grain on the Sabbath. This was considered reaping and therefore strictly forbidden.

In response, Jesus cites an earlier exception: When David and his followers were fleeing King Saul, they ate consecrated bread from God's shrine, lacking any other food (1 Sam. 21:1-6).

If a desperate need in David's time justified setting aside religious precepts, this should hold true in every age. Whenever the rules develop a life of their own and come between God and devout followers, they should be reconsidered, as "the Sabbath was made for humankind" and not vice versa. Furthermore, the "Son of Man is lord even of the Sabbath" (v. 28). In such cases, God's Messiah can redefine the rules.

In the second incident, Jesus enters the synagogue and heals a man with a withered hand (3:1-6). But first he challenges the Pharisees, raising the issue of doing good on the Sabbath. It was within the law to rescue someone whose life was in danger. But here Jesus heals a man whose condition was not life threatening.

This act of compassion manifested Jesus' power to restore and renew. But as a result of this assertion of his authority, the Pharisees begin a conspiracy with the Herodians to destroy him.

In the Epistle, Paul argues that he is not promoting *himself* in his preaching, but *Jesus Christ as Lord.* Through the lives we live and the words we speak, the light of God's glory shines in the darkness. But we face limitations as carriers of Christ's spirit—the frailty of our human existence is like that of a clay jar. Thus it is clear that what power we have must come from God.

Undoubtedly in the life in Christ we find ourselves afflicted, perplexed, persecuted, and struck down. Yet we are not crushed, forsaken, destroyed, or driven to despair (2 Cor. 4:8-9). In fact, it is these very experiences that make manifest to the world the reality of Christ as *the source of life within us.*

The call of Samuel to be a prophet of the Lord begins a series of readings associated with the life of David. Samuel is called during a time when seeing visions and "hearing the Word of the Lord" rarely occurred. After the third instance of Samuel hearing a voice in the night, Eli concludes that God is calling Samuel and tells him to answer, "Speak, Lord, for your servant is listening" (1 Sam. 3:9). The words Samuel receives are a shocking rejection of the house of Eli because of the transgressions of Eli's sons.

Eli accepts Samuel's rebuke as the will of the Lord (v. 18). Indeed, Samuel proves to have been called to be the Lord's prophet to all of Israel.

Grieved and angered, Jesus challenged the authority of the religious establishment, which valued strict observance of Jewish law over all other concerns. What religious customs and traditions contribute to your spiritual life? Following Jesus' example of justice and compassion, how can we insure that these practices continue to be life-giving and not self-serving?

Proper 5

Christ had his temptations and struggles with Satan, and that his followers do as well is all part of the Christian life. —Michael Patella.

Jesus had returned to Nazareth to retreat from the crowds that followed him and his disciples, to the extent that they didn't even have time to eat. Some thought Jesus had lost his mind, even to members of his family who sought to "restrain him" (Mk. 3:21).

Scribes from Jerusalem who questioned Jesus' authority accused him of being in league with the devil and casting out demons by the power of Beelzebul, chief of demons. If Jesus transgressed the law, then it followed that his exorcisms and other actions could not be of God.

Jesus refutes their accusation by pointing out that if Satan is divided against himself, his power is annulled. "How can Satan cast out Satan?" A house or kingdom divided against itself *cannot stand.*

A strong man (Satan) guards his property until he is overpowered by one who is stronger (Jesus the Messiah)—who plunders Satan's household. With the full power of God, Jesus has burst into the realm controlled by Satan and shattered the effects of evil.

Jesus goes on to declare that "people will be forgiven for their sins and whatever blasphemies [abuses or insults] they utter"; but blasphemy against the Holy Spirit is an "eternal sin" (v. 29) that is unforgivable.

Jesus had been filled with God's Spirit (1:10). Therefore, to accuse him of alliance with demons is to attribute the work of God to Satan. This would be a conscious denial of the goodness and grace of God's Spirit, who is present in all of Jesus' actions.

Jesus' mother and brothers were waiting to see him. So when he asks, "Who are my mother and my brothers?" he calls attention to a broader dimension of relationships. The arrival of the Kingdom of God has changed everything and overrules other loyalties. The person who *performs God's will* is the one who truly is mother or brother or sister.

In 2 Corinthians, Paul affirms the connection between the faith of Israel in the past and present. The "same spirit of faith" (4:13) that inspired the Psalmist (116:10) now enables the preaching of Paul. Through this Spirit we know that God raised Jesus from death, and will likewise raise us and bring us into his presence (v. 14).

Paul encourages the converts in Corinth, telling them not to lose heart. For while in this present life we may know affliction, *it will be merely transitory*. In our trials we need to focus on what *cannot* be seen. Our external life—our temporary shelter, or "tent"—may perish. But we know that we will have an eternal dwelling with God: "a house not made with hands, eternal in the heavens" (2 Cor. 5:1). This is our deepest consolation.

Samuel, a judge in the Old Testament, was a prophet, priest, and pivotal figure. When the elders of Israel demanded that he appoint a king to make them "like other nations" (1 Sam. 8:5), Samuel was displeased, and prayed to the Lord. He was directed to acquiesce to the people's demands, but also to warn them against putting their faith in an earthly king over God's kingship.

But despite Samuel's warnings, the people still demanded a king to "go out before us and fight our battles" (v. 20). Thus Samuel anointed Saul as Israel's first king (11:15), marking the transition from the rule of judges to that of a monarchy—a major shift in the very fabric of Israel's life.

Jesus proclaimed that his true family consists of those who do the will of God. How can we know that we truly are following the leading of God in our lives?

Proper 6

The only restrictions on Kingdom growth may be our willingness to expose our mustard-seed faith to the sunlight of the Spirit, and to allow God's life to grow in us. —H. King Oehmig.

He began to teach them many things in parables ... (Mk. 4:2).

The parable of the self-growing seed, found only in Mark, describes the growth of the Kingdom as a Divine mystery, not dependent on human effort. The farmer who plants the seed does nothing to bring about its growth. He sleeps at night and rises in the morning to discover that, seemingly without effort, the grain is ripe in due time. He then takes his sickle to harvest the crop.

The seeds of the Kingdom will produce a crop that it will be up to the disciples to reap. *It is always God who gives the growth.* The seeds that were planted long ago have now been fulfilled in Jesus. His power will ultimately be revealed, though it's now *hidden* like the process of germination.

The second parable illustrates how great things come from small and seemingly unpromising beginnings. A mustard seed is barely visible; yet the mustard plant itself grows to heights upwards of six feet, spreading over large areas. Again, we cannot explain how the Kingdom, like the mustard seed, is able to expand far beyond its original size. We can only say that it is God's work.

Jesus is declaring that the planting, the work he has begun, will *grow and sustain life.* In fact, the mustard shrub grows so large that "the birds of the air can make nests in its shade" (v. 32). The Kingdom is not only large, it is also life-giving and protective.

Jesus taught publicly in parables as his hearers were able to understand, and later explained them to his disciples in private.

Along with the parable of the sower (Mk. 4:3-9), these stories offered hope in times of persecution. For despite opposition, the seeds sown by Jesus' ministry would grow into the extravagant fullness of redeemed lives.

In today's Epistle, the Apostle Paul speaks of hope in the life to come, as well as a new way of living in the present. He calls the Corinthians to *"walk by faith, not by sight"* (2 Cor. 5:7). While we are at home for now in the body, we know we will perceive God more clearly when we are truly "home." We are assured that everything we do in this earthly life also matters for eternity (v. 10).

Paul goes on to say that the love of Christ "urges us on" because the death of Jesus was *for all;* and we have been changed forever by Christ's real presence among us. *Everything old has passed away; see, everything has become new!*

Israel's first king, Saul, was rejected due to his disobedience to the Lord (1 Sam. 13:7-14). Although this brought grief to God and to Samuel, the prophet obeyed God's command to travel to Bethlehem to anoint a new, obedient king from among the sons of Jesse.

Since Saul was still king, Samuel feared for his life if Saul discovered this. Thus the Lord told Samuel to proceed under the pretext of performing priestly duties. Out of all the sons of Jesse, the youngest, David, a shepherd, did not even seem worthy to be considered. But when the boy arrived, the Lord commanded Samuel to "Rise and anoint him; for this is the one" (16:12b).

Although David had not yet reached maturity, there was in him a potential for leadership perceived by God, as David was filled with the spirit of the Lord.

Jesus uses metaphors of the planting and the mysterious growth of seeds to describe the workings of the Kingdom of God. What seeds for growth have been planted in your life? How are these seeds being nurtured? What will the harvest be?

Proper 7

To clasp the hands in prayer is the beginning of an uprising against the disorder of the world.   —Karl Barth.

In today's Gospel story, Jesus and the disciples experience a sudden storm on the Sea of Galilee. It is evening, and Jesus is weary from teaching and dealing with controversies (Mk. 3:1–4:34). Leaving behind the crowds that have been following him, Jesus and the disciples get into a boat to go to the other side of the lake. Jesus trustingly rests his head on a pillow and falls asleep.

As they proceed across the lake, a severe windstorm suddenly arises. In the terrain of this region, the surrounding mountains act like a funnel, quickly propelling the storm onto the lake.

When high waves threaten to swamp the boat, the disciples panic: "Teacher, do you not care that we are perishing?" Jesus then rebukes the storm as if it were a demon: "Peace! Be still!" Immediately "the wind ceased, and there was a dead calm" (4:39b). As with the Word of God at creation, the spoken words of Jesus have the power to still the chaos of the storm.

Jesus asks the disciples why they are afraid: "Have you still no faith?" They have much more to learn from their master, whose true mission and identity will be more fully revealed through the Cross.

Who is this Jesus whom even the wind and sea obey? In the ancient world, the sea was considered a chaotic, fearful place, with monsters of the deep that could be subdued only by the power of God. Thus Jesus' ability to control the raging wind and waves is a sign of his Divine power. The storm itself symbolizes the forces of disruption and fear—in the world and in our lives—that are brought under subjection through God's redemptive action.

In the Epistle, Paul continues to seek reconciliation with the community at Corinth (2 Cor. 5:20). As they are all fellow workers with God, to whom he has been receptive, he reminds them (quoting from Is.

49:8) that God acted in the past to save Israel. Finally the long-awaited apex is at hand: "Now is the day of salvation!" (2 Cor. 6:2).

Although Paul has endured much physical hardship for the Gospel, he has been sustained by God's power (vv. 6-7). He here contrasts outward appearances with the richness of *the inward reality of his life in Christ* (vv. 8-10). The ongoing vitality of the Church depends on mutual reconciliation, as Paul and the Corinthians open their hearts to one another.

The Old Testament story of David and Goliath is more than the unlikely defeat of a mighty warrior at the hands of a young boy. It dramatizes the unexpected ways God works to overcome injustice and oppression.

The Israelites faced the superior Philistine army, represented by the mighty Goliath of Gath. The giant's intimidating size invoked fear as he swaggered forward and issued a challenge for one-on-one combat. The stakes were high, as the people of the loser would become the servants of the winner.

David volunteers, rejecting the use of Saul's oversized armor, and carrying only five smooth stones for his sling. But while the Philistines put their trust in their weapons and army, David places his faith in the Lord.

The story quickly reaches its dramatic conclusion in a single verse, as David uses his sling to hurl a stone and hit Goliath on the forehead, killing him instantly (1 Sam. 17:49).

This victory is truly a witness to the power of the living God to employ *the weak to overcome the powerful.* Now David, as Israel's newly anointed king (1 Sam. 15:13), will defend his people against their enemies.

These readings reveal that faith is more than intellectual conviction. What qualities characterize faith? What events in your own life have deepened as well as challenged your faith?

Proper 8

When we experience the abundance of God's grace, we can't help but take Jesus seriously. In Jesus, God has a way of transforming our dismissive laughter into tears of joy, our skepticism into speechless amazement. —Lewis Galloway.

Jesus was teaching by the Sea of Galilee when Jairus, a leader of the synagogue, came to him, fell at his feet, and begged him to come and heal his young daughter who was near death.

But as Jesus and the crowd set off for Jairus' home, a poor woman who had suffered from a hemorrhage for twelve years came up behind him. Although she had gone to several physicians, she became worse. She believed she could be healed simply by touching Jesus' clothing.

Acting with courage and initiative, the woman reached out for Jesus' cloak and was immediately restored. At the same moment, Jesus felt power leave him and asked who touched him. In fear and trembling, the woman came forward. Jesus, disregarding cultural barriers by talking to a woman in public, commended her faith, telling her to go in peace (Mk. 5:34).

As Jesus turned away, word was received that Jairus' daughter had died. Now the crowd insisted that there was no further need to trouble Jesus. But Jesus reassured Jairus: "Do not fear, only believe."

When Jesus arrived at Jairus' home, the crowd was already weeping over the death of the child. When Jesus insisted that "the child is not dead but sleeping" (v. 39), the mourners laughed at the euphemism.

Taking only Peter, James, John, and the child's parents, Jesus entered the house. He took the girl by the hand and addressed her as if he were indeed speaking to someone asleep, telling her to *get up*. These spoken words of Jesus bring about the miracle. Her life revived, the girl obeys the command. Jesus then orders that she be given something to eat, and again warns those present *not to tell anyone*.

This passage is a foretaste of the Resurrection of Jesus, affirming that *God is indeed the God of the living,* not the dead (Mk. 12:27).

There is a marked contrast in these stories. Jairus is a leader in the synagogue; while the unnamed woman is among the marginalized of society. However, both are treated with equal compassion by Jesus and demonstrate the nature of faith as *humble trust* and reliance on the grace of God.

In the Epistle, the Apostle Paul encourages the Corinthian community to be generous to those in need. Wherever he traveled, Paul called on his congregations to contribute to the needs of the other scattered churches (2 Cor. 8:7) as an opportunity to imitate Christ—who became poor "so that by his poverty you might become rich" (v. 9).

The needs of others were to be considered in relation to one's own wealth. In this act of sharing with others less fortunate, they themselves would be blessed and would find the faith of Christ dwelling in them ever more strongly.

Today's reading from 2 Samuel is David's moving lament over the deaths of King Saul and Saul's son Jonathan in battle (1:19, 25, 27). Despite the fact that the way is now open for David to become king over all Israel, he expresses his heartfelt grief at the death of Saul, who had played such a major role in Israel's history and in David's own life.

David proclaims the valor of Saul and Jonathan (v. 23b) and calls on the women of Israel to weep for them. The relationship between Jonathan and David epitomized the ideal of friendship (1 Sam. 18:1; 20:17).

Jesus said, "Do not fear, only believe." What contributes to your belief in Jesus? What are the barriers to your growth in faith? What helps you overcome doubts and fears?

Proper 9

The Father, Son, and Holy Spirit are always inviting us into their house of love. But when we are consumed by anger, harried by anxiety, and driven by impatience, we are blind and deaf to what God is actually doing in the present moment. —Brian Zahnd.

Jesus had returned from his travels to his hometown of Nazareth. On the Sabbath he went to the synagogue to teach; and as he spoke, the people were astounded by his wisdom and the "deeds of power ... being done by his hands!" (Mk. 6:2).

However, they did not know how to receive him. Although they might have heard of his remarkable healings, and others called him a prophet—here the people took offense. They knew him only as Mary's son, the carpenter, whose siblings also lived in Nazareth. Earlier Jesus' own family had been scandalized by his actions (Mk. 3:31-35).

Jesus was not surprised by the rejection in Nazareth, and quoted a familiar proverb: "Prophets are not without honor, except in their hometown, and among their own kin, and in their own house" (6:4). The people could not get beyond their preconceived idea of Jesus. And so, except for curing a few of the sick, "he could do no deed of power there" (v. 5).

Jesus began his public ministry in a synagogue (Mk. 1:21-28), and continued teaching in them. But after his rejection in Nazareth, Jesus is not shown by Mark as entering a synagogue again.

Jesus is amazed at the people's unbelief, and begins a new phase of his ministry to include Gentiles, as he moves beyond Galilee. Now he will send his disciples out in pairs to do *what he himself had been doing.*

He tells them to take only the barest necessities and to rely entirely on God's provision. They were not to waste time or energy on those who wouldn't receive them, but to shake the dust off their feet and leave—to demonstrate that *opposition to God's message would not cling to them.*

The disciples' tasks are clearly spelled out (vv. 12-13): to preach the message of repentance, perform deliverance, and heal the sick. This first mission of the Twelve is a reminder that we are to serve as God's agents in the world.

The Apostle Paul also experienced rejection when the church at Corinth questioned his status. In 2 Corinthians 12, Paul establishes his credentials by describing a personal mystical experience.

Fourteen years earlier he was "caught up to the third heaven" or Paradise (v. 2), far beyond the boundaries of normal human consciousness: "whether in the body or out of the body I do not know; God knows." There he heard things too sacred to be repeated.

After this, Paul was given a "thorn in the flesh" to keep him from being "too elated" (v. 7). Paul requested three times that God remove it—always to be told that the torment was to teach him *God's grace was all he needed.* "My grace is sufficient for you, for power is made perfect in weakness" (v. 9). Thus Paul, through his own frailties, could boldly state that "whenever I am weak, then I am strong."

In today's Old Testament passage, David is proclaimed king over all Israel and Judah after King Saul had been killed in battle (1 Sam. 31). Even when Saul was king, it was David who had done what a king was called to do (2 Sam. 5:2).

David was thirty years old when he began his forty-year reign. He captured Jerusalem, made it his capital, and "became greater and greater, for the Lord, the God of hosts, was with him" (v. 10).

Jesus sent out the Apostles to carry on his mission. Following their example, in what ways are we called to proclaim the Good News of Christ through words and actions in our own lives?

Proper 10

John's prophetic voice resounded like thunder. And like many other prophets from the past and in our own time, his words and actions live on to challenge and inspire. —Paula Franck.

Jesus had sent out the Twelve to minister in the villages surrounding Nazareth (Mk. 6:7-13). Inserted between their departure and subsequent return (6:30) we find the graphic account of the death of John the Baptist, who was arrested as Jesus began his ministry (Mk. 1:14).

Despite the fact that Jesus was not well received in his own hometown (Mk. 6:1-3), word of his miraculous works had spread throughout Galilee. Some even thought he was John the Baptist returned from the dead, or perhaps Elijah or another prophet.

Herod had thought that beheading John would end his problems with rabble-rousing prophets. But even Herod wondered if Jesus might be John the Baptist raised.

John had been arrested and put into prison by Herod Antipas, son of Herod the Great and tetrarch of Galilee. Herod's wife, Herodias, wanted revenge against the Baptist, who had questioned the legitimacy of her marriage. According to Mosaic law, a man is forbidden to marry his brother's wife while the brother is still living (Lev. 18:16).

However, the real motive behind John's arrest was likely political. John's popularity posed a potential threat to Herod's dominance in the region.

The opportunity for silencing the prophet came at a banquet in honor of Herod's birthday. After Herod's daughter delighted the guests by dancing, Herod offered to reward her, even to half his kingdom. Her mother Herodias instructed her to request "the head of John the Baptist."

We read that Herod was "deeply grieved" at this (Mk. 6:26); but he did not want to break his oath in front of his guests. Thus he ordered that John be killed and his head brought on a platter to the daughter, who gave it to her mother. Afterward, John's disciples came, took his body, and laid it in a tomb.

Just as John was murdered by the reigning political powers, so too was Jesus handed over and killed. Both Herod and later Pilate seemed reluctant to deliver the death sentences. Yet both rulers ultimately weakened and succumbed to outside pressure.

This grim outcome must have troubled the disciples that *one day they too* might be sentenced to death by those who "lord it over" others (Mk. 10:42).

In Ephesians we read of thankfulness for God's blessings through Jesus. First of these gifts is that *we were chosen by God* "before the foundation of the world to be holy and blameless before him" (1:4). Thus we could be adopted and become God's own children, just as Jesus is God's only Son.

The author goes on to spell out the further blessings of God's call. Through grace we are redeemed, and our sins forgiven, in "the mystery" of God's will (v. 9). Believers are sealed by the Holy Spirit; thus we are to give praise and glory to God.

In the Old Testament, David brings the Ark of the Covenant, a portable chest containing the tablets of the law, to Jerusalem, making the city the nation's religious as well as political center. The Ark symbolized God's presence in Israel, and now Jerusalem became the heart of the nation under David.

There was great rejoicing, and David himself "danced before the Lord with all his might" (2 Sam. 6:14), offered sacrifices, and blessed the people in God's name.

However, when David's wife Michal saw David dancing, "she despised him in her heart" (v. 16), viewing his exuberant behavior as unworthy of a king.

What sort of future do prophets such as John the Baptist—and other Spirit-filled individuals throughout history, up to our own time—challenge us to envision?

Proper 11

Whoever feels attracted to Jesus cannot adequately explain why. He must be prepared to be always correcting his image of Jesus for he will never exhaust what there is to know. Jesus is full of surprises. —Adolf Holl.

The twelve disciples have just returned from their missionary journey. Earlier Jesus had sent them out two by two with authority to proclaim repentance, heal the sick, and bring deliverance, just as Jesus himself had been doing (Mk. 6:7-13).

As they began to tell Jesus about their experiences, he perceived that they were weary from their travels—because of the crowds, they could not even find time to eat. Thus they went off in a boat to a "deserted place" to rest (v. 31).

Nonetheless, the people followed them on foot, and they had scarcely disembarked before being surrounded by eager followers. As Jesus looked at the crowd, "he had compassion for them, because they were like sheep without a shepherd" (v. 34). Here "compassion" is used in the sense of *merciful love*. The image of sheep without a shepherd reflects the Old Testament understanding of God as the people's saving shepherd.

In the intervening verses (35-52), Jesus' compassion results in the feeding of the five thousand; which is followed by the story of Jesus walking on water. In the second part of today's reading (vv. 53-56), as Jesus and the disciples again disembark, they are surrounded by throngs of people bringing him their sick. Wherever Jesus went, the response was the same. People begged to touch the fringe of his garment, and "all who touched it were healed." This contrasts starkly to his experience in Nazareth, where he "could do no deed of power" (Mk. 6:5).

Ephesians 2 speaks of *God's promise of unity* made available through Christ to everyone—Jew and Gentile alike. This new spiritual community is built on the foundation of the Apostles and prophets with Jesus as the Cornerstone.

Before Christ came, Gentiles lived beyond the hope of God's promises. Now, through Christ, the barriers between Jew and Gentile have shattered, as all are brought together in the fullness of God's peace. Now there is reconciliation with "one new humanity in place of the two" (2:15). Because of Jesus Christ, no one is a stranger or alien in God's household.

In the saga of King David, foreign enemies have been defeated and Israel is united. With his kingdom secure, David has proposed to the Prophet Nathan that the Ark of the Covenant be given a permanent home. "I am living in a house of cedar, but the ark of God stays in a tent" (2 Sam. 7:2). Initially Nathan concurred with David's plans; but at night the Lord prompted Nathan to reject David's notion of building a house for the Lord.

The Ark had gone before the Hebrews throughout their wilderness journey (Num. 10:33), as a manifestation of God's presence. Thus they had perceived God moving freely among them, and no permanent dwelling for the Ark was required. Instead, God promised to build a house for David—but in the sense of a dynasty rather than a palace.

David's enemies had been vanquished. Now the Lord promised that Israel would have its own land, secure from its enemies; and David would be given a name "like the name of the great ones of the earth" (2 Sam. 7:9). David's descendants would continue his kingdom and "build a house for my name" (v. 13). Thus the house—the dynasty—of David would continue forever in relationship with God as a son is to a father.

Acting out of compassion, Jesus responded freely to the needs of those who came to him. What are the requests you bring to Jesus in prayer? How does the presence of Christ in your life bring peace and healing?

Proper 12

The well-fed crowd doesn't exactly get it. They want a king with a scepter and a crown, chariots and horses. But Jesus is not that kind of king. He reveals that the true, transformative power of God is at its heart the power of unconditional, self-giving love. —Joanna Adams.

All four Gospels tell of Jesus' feeding of the five thousand. But John's emphasis (6:1-21) is on the disciples' growing understanding of *Jesus' power* to bring life to the world.

The crowds continued to follow Jesus as he healed the sick. Now it was almost Passover. Jesus had been seeking time alone with his disciples; but when he saw the large crowd that had traveled far to see him, he resolved to provide them food. Thus he asks Philip how they are to feed all these people—to test him, since Jesus already knew what he would do.

Philip points out that six months' wages would be needed to buy enough bread to feed everyone. Andrew then points out that a boy in the crowd has five loaves and two fish. *But what is so little when there is so much need?* Although Philip and Andrew have been with Jesus from the beginning (Jn. 1:35-51), they have not learned to look beyond ordinary expectations to realize that *Jesus will provide out of what is at hand.*

Jesus takes the bread, gives thanks, and distributes the food—customary actions at any Jewish meal, but also suggestive of the Eucharist. When the crowd is satisfied, they find there are twelve baskets of leftovers. Once again Jesus has redefined what is possible: the broken leftover fragments are more than what was on hand when the meal began.

Recalling the manna provided for the Israelites in the wilderness (Ex. 16:14-15), this story challenges our fundamental beliefs about scarcity and abundance and provides a foretaste of the Messianic banquet.

After this miracle the people want to make Jesus their king, assuming he "is indeed the prophet who is to come into the world" (Jn. 6:14). But Jesus understood that temporal kingship was not the vocation prepared for God's Messiah.

Jesus then withdrew to the mountains while the disciples set out across the Sea of Galilee, returning to Capernaum in their boat (vv. 16-17). It was dark and windy, and as the waters became turbulent, they looked up, terrified to see Jesus walking toward them across the water—until Jesus reassured them: "It is I; do not be afraid"; whereupon their boat reached shore. Ironically, the disciples are afraid of the one they least need to fear.

The Epistle also expresses complete confidence in God's unsurpassed love. The writer bows in reverence to God, "from whom every family in heaven and on earth takes its name" (Eph. 3:15). The prayer goes on to ask for the spiritual power that comes from God's indwelling Spirit through faith and love (v. 17). To be able to comprehend the breadth, length, height, and depth of this love is more important than acquiring knowledge. Through this love we may be "filled with all the fullness of God" (v. 19), which is the ultimate goal of life.

Today's Old Testament passage in 2 Samuel is the first of two readings that tell the pivotal story of King David and Bathsheba. David has been portrayed as an untarnished hero who enjoyed the favor of God; but this account of adultery and murder shows David abusing his power for selfish gain. As the Lord's anointed, he lived in God's favor; yet it is the soldier Uriah, a Hittite mercenary, who here exemplifies loyalty and honesty.

The miracles of the loaves and fish and Jesus walking on the water are two of the seven signs in the Gospel of John—stories told to deepen faith in Jesus as the Messiah. How do we understand the many layers of meaning in these stories today? How do they contribute to your faith and belief in Jesus?

Proper 13

When you take these elements of bread and wine do you understand yourself encountering the Risen Christ? —Robert Cornwall.

After the miraculous feeding of the five thousand, the crowd following Jesus still seems to desire national liberation. Aware of this misunderstanding of his mission, Jesus reminds them that bread is a perishable commodity. Even the manna of Moses in the wilderness would not keep beyond a day.

Thus Jesus declares that his hearers must not work for food of no enduring value, but for the eternal sustenance the Son of Man can provide. As God's Messiah, *Jesus himself* is that heavenly food (Jn. 6:27).

The crowd then asks Jesus what they must do to "perform the works of God" (v. 28). Jesus responds that this does not refer to *actions* but to *believing in Jesus* as the revelation sent by God. It cannot be achieved, but is to be *received* by faith.

Once again the crowd asks for a sign, as they recall the provision of manna to their ancestors in the wilderness (Ex. 16:4). Jesus reminds them that it was not Moses but *God the Father* who gave them bread from heaven. And the manna was only a temporary solution. All who ate it eventually died. In contrast, the "true bread from heaven" gives eternal life to the world. However, the crowd is still thinking of a material substance, and is astounded as Jesus proclaims: "I am the bread of life."

"Whoever comes to me will never be hungry, and whoever believes in me will never be thirsty" (v. 35b). As the bread of life, Jesus will satisfy the deep hunger of all who turn to him. The miracle here is one of *faith,* accepting the new pattern of life embodied in Jesus.

Ephesians 4 stresses that all followers of Jesus have a vocation from God, and thus are called to a life of true humility worthy of this call (vv. 1-2). We must always bear with one another in love, seeking the bond of peace that unites us.

Our individual vocations are to serve the community, since we are a single body animated and guided by the Spirit. We acknowledge "one Lord, one faith, one baptism, one God and Father of all" (vv. 5-6). All of us have been given gifts according to Christ's desire to equip the saints for ministry, for "building up the body of Christ." Thus we are to "grow up in every way into him who is the head, into Christ" (v. 15).

In the Old Testament, David faces the consequences of adultery with Bathsheba and the murder of her husband Uriah. When David married Bathsheba, and she bore him a son, it appeared as though David had successfully covered up his misdeeds. But David had displeased the Lord, who then sent the Prophet Nathan to him.

Nathan tells David a parable about two men: a rich man who had everything and a poor man who had only one beloved ewe lamb. When the rich man planned a feast, he took the poor man's only lamb, despite the fact that he had many flocks.

David is outraged at this heartlessness, and declares that such a man deserves death. In one of the most dramatic moments in Scripture, Nathan confronts David, saying, "You are the man!" (2 Sam. 12:7).

David's confession (v. 13) reveals that he still submits to God and accepts the consequences of his actions. Yet the cost of his misdeeds is high. The son born to Bathsheba dies, and David's kingdom falls prey to civil war.

As Jesus explains the deeper significance of the miracle of the feeding of the five thousand, he declares, "I am the bread of life." As you reflect on that image, how does your life in Christ provide spiritual nurture? What is the enduring value of the bread brought by Jesus?

The Transfiguration

The Transfiguration is the ultimate epiphany, the manifestation of God in human beings ... so that they become fully human, as they were meant to be.   —David M. Rhoads.

Accounts of Jesus' Transfiguration are found in Matthew, Mark, and Luke. In Luke, Peter's confession of Jesus as "the Messiah of God" (Lk. 9:20) was followed by Jesus' first prediction of his Passion (vv. 21-22) and teachings on the true cost of discipleship. The Transfiguration marks a turning point in Jesus' ministry as he begins his journey to Jerusalem.

Luke's telling is set within the context of prayer. Here Jesus takes Peter, James, and John with him up the mountain. While Jesus is at prayer, the appearance of his face changes, and his clothes become dazzling white (v. 29), an outward manifestation of his divinity.

Then Moses and Elijah appear "in glory" and talk with Jesus about his coming "departure" ("exodus") or death in Jerusalem (v. 31). Moses and Elijah converse with Jesus as representatives of the law and prophets, affirming his Messiahship. Tradition viewed the reappearance of these two prophets as a sign of the coming of the Messianic age.

In response to this vision, Peter and the others are "weighed down with sleep" (v. 32a). Later on, they would again fall asleep while Jesus prayed on the Mount of Olives before his crucifixion (22:45-46).

Peter, "not knowing what he said" (v. 33b), proposed that they erect three dwellings to memorialize the site, similar to those constructed at the harvest Feast of Booths. But this was not to be.

At this point, the disciples were terrified as they became overshadowed by a cloud. Then a voice from the cloud, similar to the one at Jesus' Baptism, proclaimed: "This is my Son, my Chosen; listen to him!"

Luke tells us that the Apostles "kept silent and in those days told no one any of the things they had seen" (v. 36). It was not until the Resurrection that they could begin to understand what they had just witnessed. Later, Peter would recall the Transfiguration as he anticipated his own death and defended his teaching on Jesus' second coming.

Peter's opponents maintained that the Apostle's teaching on the second coming of *Jesus as judge* was a "cleverly devised myth" (2 Pet. 1:16). However, Peter replied that he could proclaim with confidence this "prophetic message" (v. 19) because he was present on the holy mountain when Jesus "received honor and glory from God the Father." Peter also affirms that interpretation of Scripture is not just an individual matter; prophecy comes through men and women who were moved by God's Holy Spirit.

The Transfiguration of Jesus also recalls the experience of Moses on Mt. Sinai. After Moses came down from the mountain bearing the tablets of the law, the people were afraid because "the skin of his face shone" (Ex. 34:29). When he spoke directly with God, the reflection of God's glory, or Shekinah, remained on his face.

It was generally believed that to encounter the Divine face to face meant death, for who could bear to see the awesome majesty of God? Thus the people were afraid to come near Moses.

Once Moses realized the source of their fear, he covered his face with a veil—which he removed when he spoke with God and when he gave the word to the people. This gave an assurance of safety to the Israelites as they came near to hear what God had entrusted to their leader.

Today's readings describe encounters with the Divine that are filled with awe and mystery. Recall a time in your own life when you had an experience of incredible joy and wonder—your own "mountaintop experience." How were you changed by this event? How does this realization continue to impact your life?

Proper 14

Even as Christ invites us to this table, he does not mean for us to linger here forever. He gives us sustenance in order to send us forth, carrying a space of welcome within us, called to offer it to those we meet: one more, and one more, and one more … —Jan Richardson.

Jesus faces the hostility of the crowds when he declares that *he is the bread from heaven* who will bring eternal life to all who have faith in him. After all, they know his father Joseph and do not take seriously the idea that Jesus is God. To come from heaven and to be able to give life to others was unimaginable, and brought all Jesus' other claims into question. Yet for John the Evangelist, to recognize that Jesus was from God was *the source of faith itself.*

Jesus calls followers to refrain from complaining among themselves. He goes on to say that one does not come to him by personal effort. Instead, God initiates the response: "No one can come to me unless drawn by the Father who sent me" (Jn. 6:44).

To be taught by God is to hear and accept Jesus. Now God's teaching will come through Jesus and will be available to all who believe. No one has seen the Father except Jesus; so he is the only one who can make the Father known. And whoever believes in him has eternal life (v. 47).

The miraculous bread in the wilderness insured survival when the Hebrews faced starvation; but all those who ate the manna eventually died. Even the feeding of the five thousand provided only temporary nourishment. However, the living bread that Jesus himself offers leads to eternal life—and the restoration of all creation. "The bread that I will give for the life of the world is my flesh" (v. 51b). Jesus' gift of himself is *his very body,* which will be sacrificed at his crucifixion.

Ephesians refers to this self-giving of Christ by urging Jesus' followers to "live in love, as Christ loved us and gave himself up for us"

(5:2). The love of God becomes a reality in Christ, and those who follow Jesus must center their lives in love.

Thus the Ephesians are to speak the truth and restrain from anger, sin, and harsh words that would give opportunity to the devil—speaking "only what is useful for building up" (4:29). They are to put away bitterness, wrath, wrangling, slander, and malice. Instead they are to be "imitators of God" (5:1), worthy of their inheritance.

In the story of David, his rebellious and ambitious son Absalom had fled Israel for three years after killing his half-brother Amnon, who had raped Absalom's sister Tamar (2 Sam. 13). When he returned, David did not welcome his son home for two years. Thus Absalom began plotting to take the throne from his father. In the ensuing civil war, David was forced to leave Jerusalem.

Now the decisive battle is about to begin. David knows that Absalom and his followers are no match for David's army, and he orders his generals to "deal gently for my sake with the young man Absalom" (18:5). Absalom's forces are soundly defeated in the forest of Ephraim. As Absalom rides away, he is caught as his hair becomes entangled in a tree. Subsequently, he is killed on orders of David's trusted general, Joab.

When the news is brought to David, he is grief-stricken at his son's fate. Despite Absalom's treachery and disloyalty, David mourns his death.

In light of the images of bread in the Gospel passage, what added meaning does the phrase "Give us this day our daily bread" from the Lord's Prayer have for you? How does Jesus, as the bread that came down from heaven, bring radical changes into the world and into our lives?

Proper 15

On what do we feed? The answer is that we feed upon the very life of Christ. That is what distinguishes a Christian. —Angus Dun.

Jesus continues to explain the deeper meaning of the miraculous feeding of the five thousand as he declares: *The bread I will give for the life of the world is my flesh* (6:51); and "unless you eat the flesh of the Son of Man and drink his blood, you have no life in you." To take this literally would be to see Jesus as actual food to be consumed. This made an already difficult concept totally unacceptable to his audience: "How can this man give us his flesh to eat?"

Jewish dietary laws forbade ever consuming blood; slain animals had to be bled before consumption. Violation of these laws meant being cut off from the community (Lev. 17:14-15). So to speak of drinking human blood, even symbolically, was too terrible to contemplate.

Yet it is precisely such imagery that Jesus employs as the sole means by which a person can attain eternal life. "Those who eat my flesh and drink my blood have eternal life, and I will raise them up on the last day" (v. 54). They will abide in him and he in them (v. 56). We appropriate this "flesh and blood" through the spiritual sustenance of the Eucharist.

Jesus was sent by "the living Father" (v. 57). Just as Jesus is sustained by the Father, so his followers will have life through him.

Jesus goes on to make a distinction between "the bread that came down from heaven" and the manna of the exodus. God had preserved the community by providing sustenance; but those who ate that bread died. In contrast Jesus, the bread from heaven, gives eternal life to every individual who accepts him.

Those who consume this living bread will also participate in Jesus' relationship with the Father and his Resurrection life, for "the one who eats this bread will live forever" (v. 58). This also means sharing a new quality of life in the present.

Ephesians explains that the Christian life is to be lived as an alternative to the dominant culture. "Be careful then how you live ... because the days are evil" (5:15-16). The writer goes on to point out the temptations that surround believers; thus they are not to be foolish but to understand the will of God for them.

Christians are called to a Spirit-filled life of moderation and sobriety. If they are to manifest God's purposes in the world, there is no place for self-indulgent excesses that would detract from their witness. The presence of God in their lives will be manifested in communal praise and thanksgiving.

In today's Old Testament passage, King Solomon asks the Lord for gifts of understanding and discernment in order to govern wisely. When David, the most celebrated king in Israel's history, died after a reign of forty years (1 Ki. 2:10), the throne of Israel was inherited by his son Solomon, who in turn reigned for forty years. During this time, Solomon increased the wealth and international political influence of Israel; built the temple at Jerusalem; and gained a reputation for great wisdom (4:30)—a fulfillment of the request he made of God.

Although Solomon loved the Lord, "walking in the statutes of his father David" (3:3), he also went to the high places to offer sacrifices, which was considered a pagan act. Thus Solomon disregarded his own prayer for wisdom and disobeyed the Lord's commandments.

As we share the bread and the cup, we abide in Jesus and he in us. Thus we participate fully in his life, death, and Resurrection. How are we, as the Body of Christ, called to live in the light of this relationship?

Proper 16

When Jesus said, "I am the bread of life," he must have meant he was scattering bits of himself like a trail of crumbs leading us to speak and act and scatter forgiveness in his name to the ends of the earth. —Susan Springer.

Jesus continues to explain the miracle of the feeding of the multitude: "Those who eat my flesh and drink my blood abide in me, and I in them" (Jn. 6:56). He is the living bread that came down from heaven, and whoever eats *this* bread—unlike the ancestors who ate the manna in the desert—*will live forever.* This is an invitation to participate fully in Jesus' life, death, and Resurrection by believing in him—*taking him into ourselves.*

But many who heard this were offended, taking it too literally. To them, these concepts were impossibly scandalous. But even those who grasped that images of flesh and blood represented *sharing fully in the life of Jesus* found its practice difficult.

Jesus, aware of his own disciples' misgivings, asks: "What if you were to see the Son of Man ascending to where he was before?"—that is, returning to God as did the great spiritual leaders of the past. Would they then be more likely to accept his hard sayings? But Jesus doesn't need to demonstrate this. Because he was with God in the beginning (Jn. 1:2), *he comes from there;* thus his words have ultimate authority.

None of this is meant to degrade the flesh, for Jesus is the Word made flesh (Jn. 1:14); but life in the flesh will not endure. However, the words that Jesus brings are *spirit* and *life*—and the enlivening power of the Spirit is eternal.

Jesus knew there were those who would not believe him, as well as one who would ultimately betray him. Thus he warns "no one can come to me unless it is granted by the Father" (v. 65). As always, some will close their hearts to God's invitation. Thus many of the Lord's followers abandoned him.

Jesus then turns to the Twelve to ask if they too wish to leave. Speaking for the others as well, Peter affirms that *there is nowhere else to go,* for they "have come to believe and know that you are the Holy One of God" (v. 69) who gives eternal life.

This then is the meaning of the feeding of the five thousand. Eating and drinking are *metaphors for fully participating in the life of Jesus;* and the call to follow Christ includes difficult and seemingly impossible demands. Yet to accept Jesus as the true bread from heaven is to find in him the climactic revelation of God that leads to everlasting life.

In Ephesians, believers are instructed to put on "the whole armor of God" (6:11) in order to withstand the powers of evil. It is the strength of God's power—not human willpower—that will overcome these cosmic forces as the followers of Jesus stand and proclaim the "mystery of the gospel" (v. 19).

The Old Testament passage in 1 Kings 8 is taken from the dedication of the temple in Jerusalem, as King David's dream to build a house for the Lord becomes a reality. David had brought the Ark of the Covenant to Jerusalem; but it was left to Solomon, his heir, to build a temple to house the Ark. Although God is present in all places, and cannot be contained in a building, the temple offered a place for the prayers of all who entered. David's successors would remain on the throne of Israel only as long as the people remembered to follow the Lord's commandments.

Jesus' teachings challenge us to see the world differently—to look beyond the surface to underlying layers of meaning in his words. How are our lives changed when we open our hearts and minds to the mystery of the Gospel?

Proper 17

Deep in the recesses of our minds and hearts lies the hidden treasure that we once had and now seek. We know its preciousness, and we know that it holds the gift we most desire: a spiritual life stronger than physical death. —Henri Nouwen.

As the Gospel readings return to Mark, we read in chapter 7 how scribes and Pharisees from Jerusalem accuse Jesus' disciples of disregarding established religious customs. Some of them did not wash their hands before eating, and by "eating with defiled hands" (Mk. 7:2) they were ignoring the oral tradition of the elders.

Jesus was known to be skilled at rabbinic arguments. Thus, in response to the Pharisees' question about why his disciples ate with defiled hands (v. 5), Jesus quotes Isaiah 29:13: "This people honors me with their lips, but their hearts are far from me ... " (v. 6b). They have abandoned God's commandments in order to observe often empty human rituals.

Jesus did not come to abolish the law or the way of life defined by Moses. The Pharisees valued ritual purity as a preservation of Jewish identity in the wider culture; but for many the practices had become an end in themselves.

For instance, honoring one's parents, which included the obligation to support them if necessary, was often disregarded in favor of supporting the temple. Jesus condemns the use of religious precepts to ignore compassionate moral responsibilities.

Jesus then turns from the Pharisees to the crowd, and moves from the issue of observance of ritual to *what constitutes defilement* (vv. 14-15). It is not what enters a person from outside, such as food, that has the power to corrupt; rather it is what comes *from within.*

Jesus emphasizes that it is "from the human heart" that evil intentions come (v. 21), and then lists the vices that defile—forces within us that separate us from God and others. Thus Jesus calls his followers not to be so concerned with *external* practices that they neglect justice and righteousness.

Today's reading in James begins with a reminder that every gift comes from God. We have been given a new birth by the word of truth, and thus are connected to Christ as "first fruits" of God's creation (1:18). This is the basis for all behavior toward others. Thus we are to be slow to anger, for "your anger does not produce God's righteousness" (v. 20); and we are to resist wicked and sordid behavior.

Blessings come from being "doers of the word, and not merely hearers who deceive themselves" (v. 22). James goes on to point out that pure and undefiled religion calls us to *care for those in need,* such as widows and orphans, and to stay unstained by the world (v. 27). It is inauthentic to claim that we have heard God's Word unless we follow through and act on it in our lives.

Today's Old Testament reading is from Song of Solomon (2:8-13). This collection of sensual love poems between a woman and her lover, perhaps intended for wedding celebrations, has parallels in other ancient Near Eastern writings. In the Jewish tradition, the Song of Solomon is used in the Passover observance, and is interpreted allegorically as illustrating the love of God for Israel. Some Christians see it as a reflection of Christ's love for the Church.

Whether read literally or allegorically, Song of Solomon celebrates the renewing power of love—human and Divine. Just as these lovers joyfully dwell in mutual love, we too are invited to celebrate our love for God.

Following the Gospel means discerning what is essential to true faith and what is not—becoming doers and not just hearers of the Word. What contributes to authentic religious practice and ethical living, both in the Church and in our own lives? What are you called to do as you hear the words of Jesus?

Proper 18

Blessed are they who ask for no miracles, demand nothing out of the ordinary, but who find God's message in everyday life. —Romano Guardini.

When Jesus arrived in Tyre, he sought privacy; but reports of his fame had spread, and "he could not escape notice." Suddenly a Gentile woman, a Syrophoenician, bowed before Jesus and begged him to heal her daughter of an "unclean spirit." At first, Jesus harshly denied her request. He had come to feed the children (Jews) and not the dogs (Gentiles). But the woman continued to press her case, since even dogs are allowed leftovers. She did not challenge the priority of the Jews, but petitioned for Gentiles as well.

Jesus then acquiesced to the woman's argument, declaring that her daughter had been healed. The deliverance took place instantaneously and from a distance. When the woman returned home, her child was lying in bed, restored.

This is the only time in Mark's Gospel that Jesus seems to be "bested" in an argument. This woman stood her ground and used Jesus' own words to her advantage. *The "dogs" under the table were already sharing the children's bread.* But soon they would cease to be considered dogs and become recognized as children alongside the chosen.

The focus here is not so much on deliverance as on breaking down boundaries of geography, gender, ethnicity, and religious purity—in order to extend the Kingdom of God *to all who would receive it.*

In the second story, a deaf man with a speech impediment was brought to Jesus for healing. Jesus performed most of his works in public view. However, here he took the man aside, and the procedure was more complex. Jesus put his fingers in the man's ears, then spat and touched his tongue (Mk. 7:33). On two other occasions Jesus used saliva as a healing agent (Mk. 8:23; Jn. 9:6), transforming a gesture of insult and abasement into a means of healing.

After gazing into heaven, Jesus uttered *"Ephphatha"*—an Aramaic word that Mark translates as "Be opened." At this demonstration of the power of the word, the man was healed. Now he could hear and speak plainly.

Immediately, Jesus cautions the witnesses to this event to tell no one. Yet such warnings did little to silence news of his miracles—they announced that *Jesus does all things well.* Thus God's reign proclaims itself.

The Epistle calls attention to right treatment of the poor, and the need to obey the commandments. First there is the reminder that God's acceptance of all who have faith must be honored also in the Christian community. True believers in Christ should show no partiality to the worldly rich and powerful. In truth, God has "chosen the poor in the world to be rich in faith and to be heirs of the kingdom ... " (Jas. 2:5). In contrast, the rich bring oppression and blasphemy.

Verses 14-17 express the demand for action that is central to the Epistle of James. Thus if love toward a neighbor in need fails to prompt the active relief of that need, one's profession is meaningless. A claim to faith that does not result in a concrete response is dead (v. 17). It is by our actions that our faith becomes manifested in the world.

Proverbs is a compilation of sayings designed to teach moral values to young people. The passage for today also calls attention to God's care for the marginalized, and challenges the assumption that people with material wealth have been favored by God—as the Lord is the maker of us all (22:2).

What cultural, social, economic, and religious barriers are we called to overcome in order to live into the vision of God's Kingdom? What can faith communities do to respect the dignity of every human being and make all people, regardless of their circumstances, feel welcome? What will be your own part in this endeavor?

Proper 19

The loving Jesus did not come with Band-Aids and antibacterial ointment; he came as God's word, and the healing balm was painful truth, and the promise was that out of this truth we would be set free.   —Geralyn Wolf.

In the Gospel, Jesus makes the first of three pronouncements about his coming Passion (Mk. 8:31). As Jesus and his disciples continue their travels in the Gentile territory of Caesarea Philippi, Jesus raises a central theme of the Gospel: "Who do people say that I am?"

The disciples reply that some people identify him with John the Baptist. John had proclaimed that God's reign was about to begin, and only repentance could protect people from the impending judgment. Jesus also preached God's coming Kingdom and the need for repentance, so his ministry could be seen as a continuation of John's.

Some referred to Jesus as Elijah, who reportedly had been seen going "up to heaven" in a whirlwind (2 Ki. 2:11)—and whose return would herald the advent of the Messiah. Had he been sent back to earth to prepare for Jesus' coming?

Then the inquiry becomes more personal as Jesus asks the disciples: "But who do *you* say that I am?" Peter confidently speaks for all of them as he declares, "You are the Messiah" (Mk. 8:29).

But Jesus sternly orders them to tell no one. First they must be led into a new understanding of *what it means* that Jesus is the Messiah. Moreover, to proclaim this posed a danger of reprisals from Roman and Jewish authorities.

Jesus tells them quite openly that he is about to endure great suffering and be rejected before his death and ultimate Resurrection. The life of the Messiah is not just about miraculous healings and events. And instead of seeking political or military triumph, Jesus will sacrifice himself.

The disciples cannot grasp or accept the reality of a suffering Messiah—a concept completely at odds with the expectations on which

Peter and the others had set their hopes. Thus Peter pulls Jesus aside and rebukes him, inviting an equally strong response from Jesus in front of the other disciples: "Get behind me, Satan!" It would be tempting for Jesus to seek to avoid suffering, but that would be to submit to human rather than Divine purposes.

Then Jesus tells both the disciples and the crowd that those who would follow him must "deny themselves and take up their cross" (v. 34). This is a *voluntary act:* living selflessly and bringing Jesus' message to a suffering world.

Jesus' example of self-abandonment actually underlines that—paradoxically—*to gain one's life is to lose it* (vv. 35-37). To share in Jesus' death also means to take part in his Resurrection.

James also speaks of living in a manner acceptable to God. The tongue—the power of the spoken word—represents all that must be controlled in human nature. There is potential for great harm if teachers proclaim false doctrine; thus they "will be judged with greater strictness" (3:1). At the heart of faithful response to God is integrity; and undisciplined speech poses a threat to the community.

In Proverbs, the underlying assumption is that God has given humankind the ability to discern right choices: "The fear of the Lord is the beginning of knowledge; fools despise wisdom and instruction" (1:7).

In today's reading, Woman Wisdom makes her grand entrance with a loud shout, as she goes into the busy city streets and calls the people to heed her and abandon their foolish ways. Those who follow the paths of Wisdom "will be secure and will live at ease, without dread of disaster" (v. 33).

What is your response to Jesus' question: "Who do you say that I am?" What led you to this understanding? What are the challenges and blessings of following Jesus—what might you need to give up in your life in order to save it?

Proper 20

Jesus isn't interested in who we *say* is the greatest or even in who acts like the greatest or looks to be great. Jesus is interested in who acts with the greatest grace, compassion, and love. —Amy Allen.

Jesus has nearly completed his public ministry. Now his main concern is not winning new disciples, but teaching those already committed to him. Although the Twelve have seen his miraculous acts and listened to his teaching, their minds are still set on human rather than Divine things (Mk. 8:33).

In today's reading we find the second and shortest of Mark's three Passion predictions (8:31; 9:31; 10:33-34). Once again, the disciples fail to grasp Jesus' warning of his coming betrayal, death, and Resurrection. Jesus' teachings have full meaning only in light of his Passion.

The disciples *still* identify the Messiah as a victor who will establish a glorious future; but they think of this only in worldly terms. After they recognized Jesus as Messiah, they were confronted with the shocking prospect of *a willing sacrifice*—which signified to them complete failure. Too fearful and confused to ask Jesus to explain, they began to argue among themselves over who was the greatest.

Yet even as they vied for positions of honor, the disciples had some idea that they had missed the mark—when they contrasted Jesus' denial of self with their own desire for reward.

But for Jesus, the only way to be *first in God's eyes* is to choose to be last of all—that is, to consider the needs of others before self. "Whoever wants to be first must be last of all and servant of all" (9:35). With this radical statement. Jesus turns cultural assumptions about power and status upside down.

To illustrate this, Jesus presents and embraces a young child—powerless, defenseless, and reliant on others—someone with no legal rights. There would be no gain in receiving a child. But to be *as vulnerable as a child* is to be open to the power of love—the central teaching of Jesus. Whoever receives such a child in his name *receives Christ himself,* as well as Abba the Father who sent him (v. 37).

So who is wise and understanding? Who truly *is* the greatest? In the paradoxical logic of God's Kingdom, it is the one who follows the example of Jesus as the humble servant of all—open to his transforming love.

The Book of James also offers conclusions about *who truly is wise* by contrasting the dangers of worldly wisdom based on *desire* with the benefits of heavenly wisdom built on *peace.*

True wisdom is pure and peaceable, without partiality or hypocrisy. It is manifested through living a good life, with works that are "done with gentleness born of wisdom" (3:13b). All who seek this way of wisdom and compassion will find that it yields the fruits of serenity, mercy, kindness, and assurance of God's presence. Therefore we are to resist the devil and dwell near to God, who will also draw close to us.

The reading from Proverbs contains verses in praise of "a capable wife" (31:10). However, on a deeper level, the essence of personified Wisdom as described throughout Proverbs is also conveyed here. The good wife is intelligent and of unsurpassed virtue, one who consistently and faithfully brings honor to her husband.

She looks with confidence to the future (v. 25b), and is wise and kind. Consequently, her children love her, and her husband praises her. Finally, this woman of strength "fears the Lord" (v. 30), and is a living representative of Wisdom.

What are some of the attributes of faithful discipleship? In particular, what does it mean to be a "servant of all"? How can we practice serving one another with love and gentle wisdom?

Proper 21

Discipleship involves discovering a new family and a rich life within the community of those who have been grasped by the grace of God and have learned the joy of spending themselves on others. —Donald H. Juel.

The inner circle of Jesus' disciples pondered how to relate to outsiders who reportedly cast out demons in his name. Jesus' success in deliverance had been such that the very invocation of his name was believed to have healing properties.

Jesus' response reveals his lack of concern, reaffirming that *those who are not explicitly disciples can still do God's work* (Mk. 3:31-35). What matters is that God's purposes are being fulfilled and people set free. No one can claim to own the name of Jesus; instead, *Jesus owns those who call on his name.* "Whoever is not against us is for us" (9:40).

The community of Jesus' followers is to include everyone. Unless there is reason to believe that someone poses a negative threat, they should accept those doing good in Jesus' name. Whoever does the smallest service for a follower of Jesus shall surely be rewarded.

Jesus also calls the disciples to examine their own behavior, warning that anyone causing believers—"these little ones" (v. 42)—to turn away from following him *will bring destruction on themselves.* It would be better to die than to be the cause of another person's ruin—even to be thrown into the sea with a heavy millstone around one's neck.

Any actions preventing others from following God's will *must be renounced* (vv. 43-47). These exaggerated suggestions of cutting off a hand or foot, or tearing out an eye, are not to be taken literally. Yet they warn us to *rid ourselves of whatever prevents wholehearted devotion to God.*

The word translated "stumble" in these verses means "to take offense" or "to scandalize." To put an obstacle in the way of another person's faith is a very serious matter indeed—one of hellish consequence. This is not a strict dogma of eternal damnation. However, to be "thrown into hell" meant at the very least to suffer the pain of being excluded from the community.

The passage concludes with several sayings about salt. First Jesus warns of future trials and persecutions the disciples will face when "everyone will be salted with fire" (v. 49). These hardships will be like a purifying fire. Believers are not to lose their passion and zeal, or they will become like salt that has lost its taste. They must find mutual peace in order to face the challenges ahead.

In the conclusion to the Book of James (5:13-20), the author affirms the power of joyful prayer to transform all aspects of life, including bringing healing to the sick and forgiveness to sinners. Despite the difficulties and temptations that assail us as we try to follow Christ, we know that in the community of faith *there is salvation.*

The Book of Esther, probably written between 400 and 300 B. C., tells the story of a woman who acted boldly and whose actions saved the Jewish people. Though God is not directly mentioned, it is clear in the narrative that *the Lord acts on behalf of God's people.* The story of Esther also provides the origin of the Jewish festival of Purim, the only major holy day on the Jewish calendar not mandated in the Torah.

Esther put her own life at risk by pleading with the king to save her people (7:3-4); and her courage in laying down her life in this dramatic way is a model for the marginalized and powerless in all times who triumph over great odds.

What are some of the stumbling blocks in your spiritual life that interfere with wholehearted devotion to God? How are you striving to overcome these obstacles?

Proper 22

**Marriage is not a problem to be solved. It is a mystery to be lived.
—Charles Hoffacker.**

In today's Gospel, the Pharisees "test" Jesus by asking if it is lawful for a man to divorce his wife. But instead of answering, Jesus responds with another question: "What did Moses command you?" (Mk. 10:3).

The Pharisees knew that divorce was allowed as a common practice. The Torah states that a man may divorce his wife simply by handing her a certificate of divorce and dismissing her (Dt. 24:1-4). Sometimes sexual infidelity was considered a justifiable cause; but often even minor provocations could provoke a divorce.

Jesus tells them that the law on divorce was written because of their hardness of "heart"—the center of judgment and human understanding. Although Jewish law permitted a man to divorce his wife, a woman was not allowed to divorce her husband. However, after receiving a divorce certificate, she would be allowed to marry again.

Now Jesus turns from divorce to teach about marriage. While the Pharisees' main concerns are legal issues, Jesus points beyond the law to *what God intended for marriage* in the created order (Mk. 10:6-8). God's design calls for human beings to dwell in relation with God and each other. Marriage is to reflect lifelong mutuality between two individuals, and not domination of one person over another: "Therefore what God has joined together, let no one separate" (v. 9).

Although divorce is possible in a legal sense, Jesus calls attention to the pain of broken bonds between two people. Spouses were not to treat each other as property to be cast aside. Within the context of Jesus' overall teachings, marriage is to be a model of loving, faithful relationship within God's creation.

After this, the disciples attempt to prevent people from bringing children to him. Jesus indignantly rebukes them, saying, "it is to such as these that the kingdom of God belongs" (v. 14), as he takes the children into his arms and blesses them.

The Epistle today begins a series of readings from Hebrews. The prologue in 1:1-4 reflects one of the major themes of the book: *Jesus as the exalted Christ,* the ultimate revelation of God. Whereas God spoke through the prophets in former times, now God speaks through the Son, who is "the reflection of God's glory and the exact imprint of God's very being." Because of Jesus' sacrifice of himself for sins, he sits at the "right hand of God," superior to the angels and all other beings.

The Son, through his Incarnation, became for a while "lower than the angels" (2:9), thus exalting humanity. By tasting death on our behalf, he opened salvation to all and was made perfect through his suffering. Being fully human, he was not ashamed to call us brothers and sisters, with God as our Father.

The Old Testament passage is the first of four readings from the Book of Job. In a conversation before the Lord among heavenly beings, we see Satan, or the Adversary, declaring that Job, a righteous man, is faithful to God only because he prospers. Satan as "prosecutor" is allowed to test Job to see if he will blaspheme the Lord. However, even when Job loses his possessions and children, he "still persists in his integrity" (2:3).

Satan then declares that Job will not be able to withstand physical afflictions without turning against God. When these come, Job's wife asks why he doesn't curse God and die. Job replies that one must accept the bad along with the good; and still he refrains from sin.

The words and actions of Jesus give us a vision of human relationships as they should be *in God's creation. As Jesus blesses the children, what do we learn about receiving the Kingdom of God?*

Proper 23

The consequence of God's entering the realm of humanity through the person of God's son Jesus is that God has become approachable in a new way.   —L. Ann Jervis.

In the Gospel passage, a man comes to Jesus asking what to do to inherit eternal life (Mk. 10:17-22). He kneels before Jesus and calls him "Good Teacher." Jesus replies that "No one is good but God alone."

In response, Jesus summarizes six of the Ten Commandments that pertain to relationships in the community. It is the *spirit* underlying the Commandments, not the *letter,* that is *the path to life with God.* The man has kept these laws from his youth; but he is not satisfied that this is enough.

We read that Jesus looked at him and "loved him." Then he told him to sell his possessions and give the money to the poor, in order to receive "treasure in heaven" (v. 21). But Jesus intends more than obligatory almsgiving. He is asking the man to give up all his possessions, and, unencumbered, to "come, follow me."

At this, the man responds in shock and leaves, grieving, "for he had many possessions" (v. 22). This is the only mention in the Gospels of such a rejection. The man's possessions had come to possess him.

Next Jesus explains the relationship between wealth and service to God. True spiritual commitment is virtually impossible for those who are rich and overvalue possessions. Wealth itself is not a barrier to salvation; but living primarily for worldly security prevents undivided loyalty to God. Jesus adds the exaggerated image of a camel trying to get through the eye of a needle.

The disciples were "astounded"—since it was believed that riches signified God's favor. Bewildered, they ask who then *can* be saved? Jesus answers: "for God all things are possible" (v. 27). It is God who initiates salvation through grace and allows entry to the Kingdom.

In the final section, Peter speaks for all the disciples who, unlike the rich man, have forsaken everything for the sake of Jesus and the

Gospel (Mk. 1:16-20). Jesus assures them that this renunciation will be rewarded a hundredfold, though not without hardships; and "in the age to come eternal life" (v. 30).

The final verse (v. 31) is a reminder of the reversal of values in God's Kingdom, where many who expect to be first will end up last; and those who believe they will be last, are first.

Hebrews provides assurance of God's presence through the sacrifice of Christ Jesus, who fully identifies with our humanness. The living word of God is "sharper than any two-edged sword" (4:12), and everything about us is open to God's sight.

Yet we need not fear, with Jesus as our High Priest. He sympathizes with our weaknesses as one who also was tested, but is without sin.

Jesus has led the way to heaven, where we will someday follow. Thus we can "approach the throne of grace with boldness" (v. 16) to find mercy and hope in time of need.

We revisit Job after his loss of his family and possessions. Here (ch. 23) he responds to his "friend" Eliphaz, who concludes that Job committed serious misdeeds, or a just God would not have punished him so severely. If Job will only repent of his sins, God will hear and answer him.

As Job, covered with painful sores, sits in the ashes, he laments the absence of the Lord and protests his innocence. Job is not only unable to find God; he also cannot perceive God's purposes in these events.

What is the relationship between material possessions and service to God and God's Kingdom? How are we challenged when Jesus turns conventional attitudes about wealth and financial security upside down? What does it mean that those who are first will be last and the last will be first?

Proper 24

Life has its dark places where there seems to be nothing to do but hold on. Faith is always a *victory,* the victory of the soul which tenaciously maintains its clutch on God.   —William Barclay.

Ever since Jesus' predictions of his Passion (Mk. 8:31; 9:31; 10:33-34), he had been telling the disciples that his work was not sovereignty—but *sacrifice.* Yet they cannot grasp this—or the nature of their own call to God's service.

Following Jesus' third and final Passion prediction, James and John ask for favored status in the Kingdom: "Grant us to sit, one at your right hand and one at your left, in your glory" (Mk. 10:37).

This mirrors Mark 9:31-36, when the disciples argued over who was the greatest. However, then they were disputing who had preeminence during Jesus' earthly ministry. Jesus said they did not know what they were asking. "Are you able to drink the cup that I drink, or be baptized with the baptism that I am baptized with?" This referred to their sharing in the Messiah's coming sacrificial death.

James and John once again show their misunderstanding when they confidently reply that they are able to drink this cup; however, at the time of Jesus' arrest and crucifixion, they will desert him (Mk. 14:50). Jesus responds that they may share the cup he will drink, but "to sit at my right hand or at my left" is not his to grant. Only God the Father can decide this.

The other disciples are enraged by the presumption of James and John. Then Jesus addresses all of them concerning true leadership. In a society that prized power, status, and honor, they were to take a different path—one of servant leadership, not privilege. Those who adopt the values of this world ultimately can do nothing to transform it.

The truly great person is the one who provides for the welfare of others—and is ready to be the slave of all. In God's Kingdom the quest for individual power and status is to be replaced by humility and service, since Jesus "came not to be served but to serve" (10:45a).

Moreover, the Son of Man came "to give his life a ransom for many" (v. 45b). Jesus' true greatness can be understood only through his Passion and Resurrection—as the perfect example of fulfilled servanthood.

Hebrews further explains Christ's sacrifice on behalf of others. Mortal priests receive their call from God as they offer sacrifices for sins—their own as well as others'. Jesus fulfills the Father's redeeming purpose that he should be High Priest. In the Old Testament, the patriarch Abram, after rescuing his nephew Lot and his family, received a blessing from Melchizedek, a "priest of God Most High"; whereupon Abram paid a tithe to Melchizedek (Gen. 14:17-20).

Melchizedek's priesthood was without beginning or end. In Jesus, this eternal priesthood was fulfilled because of his obedience to the Father. Having been made perfect, Jesus became the source of salvation for all who would obey him (Heb. 5:9).

In the continuing story of Job's troubles, God finally speaks (ch. 38). Throughout Job's ordeal of great personal loss and affliction, he insists on his innocence and demands a hearing with God. But God has been silent.

Now God speaks out of the whirlwind, expressing the greatness displayed in all creation. No human can envision such a scenario, much less claim to understand or have taken part in its creation.

Job begins to realize that his life is part of a vast pattern of events beyond what any mortal can comprehend. No human is in a position to call the wisdom of God into question.

In our lives today, what does it mean to share the "Cup" and Baptism of Jesus? What sacrifices might we be called on to make? What assumptions about leadership, power, and authority are called into question by Jesus?

Proper 25

We have only to listen to our heart. Then the Spirit calls for us until we find our way, out of the dead-end of worry, and back to the broad and bright streets of hope. —Steven Charleston.

Jesus and his disciples were part of a large crowd leaving the city of Jericho. Suddenly the blind beggar Bartimaeus, son of Timaeus cried out, "Jesus, Son of David, have mercy on me!" (Mk. 10:47). He must have known Jesus' reputation as a healer; but the people around him did not want to be bothered and ordered him to be quiet.

However, Bartimaeus would not be silenced, and he shouted even more loudly. The phrase "Son of David" is a messianic reference (Mk. 12:35-37); and while Jesus had previously refused such a title (8:30), he does not prevent Bartimaeus from using it here.

So Jesus stopped and said, "Call him here." Now the crowd encouraged Bartimaeus: "Take heart; get up, he is calling you." And immediately he threw off his cloak, sprang up, and came to Jesus. Bartimaeus readily abandons his only possession to respond to the Lord. His cloak, which was useful in collecting coins, may also represent the way of life he is leaving behind.

Jesus then asks Bartimaeus: "What do you want me to do for you?" Bartimaeus' simple request is for restored sight: "My teacher, let me see again."

Jesus assures him that his faith has made him well. In contrast to a previous healing of a blind man (Mk. 8:22-26), this healing is instantaneous, without touch or further words.

This miracle, along with other healings of marginalized people in the Gospels, bears out Jesus' saying that *the first shall be last and the last first*—as the lowly and powerless are granted a prominent place in the Kingdom Jesus brings. Now Bartimaeus will follow Jesus in his way of obedience and faith.

Jesus' compassionate healing act may help other followers understand that Jesus' mission is a call to service and sacrifice rather than prestige or power. Perhaps even the disciples' spiritual blindness also will eventually be overcome.

The Gospel theme of a new way of seeing is reflected in the Old Testament reading, with Job's declaration that "I had heard of you by the hearing of the ear, but *now my eye sees you*" (42:5). To have one's eyes opened, both literally and figuratively, is a manifestation of God's grace.

The series of readings from Job now concludes, as Job makes his final response to God. Throughout his ordeals, all Job asks is the opportunity to bring his case directly before God. Thus, when God finally speaks, Job begins to understand that there is greater transcendent purpose and order in God's created universe than he can comprehend (v. 3b).

In the end, God does not directly answer Job's questions. But Job, through direct encounter with the Divine, finds his eyes are opened to new perspectives. Ultimately, to be human is to be vulnerable to suffering; and as mere mortals of dust and ashes, we can never truly grasp all of God's ways.

In Hebrews 7, we are offered a vision of the priesthood of Jesus. Unlike the Levitical priests who lived, served, died, and were buried, Jesus "holds his priesthood permanently, because he continues forever" (v. 24). As our Great High Priest, he is our intercessor who is without sin and "exalted above the heavens" (v. 26). Unlike earthly priests who must offer sacrifices first for their own sins, and then for the transgressions of others—Jesus has paid the price for all.

God calls us to new ways of seeing. What do you think are your spiritual blind spots? How do you bring these gaps and shortcomings to Jesus in prayer?

All Saints' Day

Unbind our hearts where love stops short and let us go to love every single neighbor near or far. Unbind our resources and let those who have much share their bounty. Unbind our spirits and let us go crying out with all the church that Jesus is Lord.
—Adam J. Copeland.

On this All Saints' Day, we are assured of God's providence in the world today and in the life to come. In the Wisdom of Solomon we read that "the souls of the righteous are in the hand of God" (3:1). They are now at peace, and any suffering they endured was like a purifying fire. God's holy ones will abide forever in truth, grace, and mercy.

The vision of the new Jerusalem (Rev. 21:1–22:5) in the Book of Revelation gives a description of life in the coming age when "death will be no more" (21:4). This work of reconciliation will also result in the renewal of all creation: "a new heaven and a new earth." In this view the Holy City of Jerusalem has been restored—like a bride adorned for her husband.

In the new age, God will dwell among mortals—consoling them, wiping every tear from their eyes (v. 4a). And this is a *present* as well as a future reality. God will make all things new from the beginning to the end.

The Gospel is on the raising of Lazarus (Jn. 11:1-44), which took place as Jesus made his way to Jerusalem. As the last of John's seven signs, it sets the stage for the plot to crucify Jesus, and for his coming Resurrection.

Bethany was the home of Jesus' friends Mary, Martha, and Lazarus. Jesus had received word from the sisters asking him to come, as their brother Lazarus was very ill. Although Jesus loved them, he delayed going for two days. Since a return to Jerusalem entailed danger for Jesus, the disciples had tried to prevent his departure. By the time Jesus finally arrived in Bethany, Lazarus had been dead for four days.

Martha came out to meet Jesus, saying Lazarus would not have died if Jesus had come sooner. Jesus assured her that her brother would rise again, and not just in the general end-time resurrection. Then Jesus declared *himself* to be the Resurrection and the Life for all who had faith in him (v. 25). Martha affirmed that she had such faith.

A tearful Mary also knelt at Jesus' feet and expressed the same regret over Jesus' timing. We see Jesus, "greatly disturbed in spirit and deeply moved," weeping as he approaches the tomb. Those present note his love for Lazarus, but question his inaction—since previously he was able to heal a man born blind (Jn. 9:13-41).

As Jesus asks to have the entrance stone removed, Martha protests that decomposition would have already begun. Lazarus has been in the cave four days, and he is truly dead. But Jesus reassures Martha that if she believes, she will see "the glory of God."

As the stone is removed, Jesus' audible prayer is not one of petition—but praise that *God is already bringing life from death*. Then Jesus commands, "Lazarus, come out!"

As Lazarus emerges from the tomb, he is fully alive and apparently completely restored. Jesus calls for his friends to finish the healing he has initiated: to unbind Lazarus and let him resume his life in the community.

As the Son of the Father with whom he is one, Jesus brings new life. He is indeed the Resurrection and the Life as he claimed. The coming death and Resurrection of Jesus will bring the gift of eternal life to the world.

On this celebration of All Saints' Day, who are some of the people that have served as models of faith and inspiration for you? How have they made a difference in your life?

Proper 26

It is in the everyday rhythms of life that the church most needs to talk about Jesus' power as the resurrection and the life. —Gail R. O'Day.

After Jesus' triumphal entry into Jerusalem, the religious authorities continued seeking excuses to denounce him. One of the scribes asked Jesus: "Which commandment is the first of all?" (Mk. 12:28b)—from among the 613 precepts of the law.

In response, Jesus quotes from the Shema (Dt. 6:4-9), a prayer recited daily by pious Jews as a central confession of faith. There is only one God whom the faithful are to love with their entire being: heart, soul, mind, and strength—worshiping God *with all that they are and all that they have.*

Jesus adds a second commandment, to "love your neighbor as yourself" (v. 31; Lev. 19:18). Love of neighbor, including positive action, is grounded in and a response to wholehearted devotion to God.

The original context of this law was to warn against holding grudges or taking vengeance against a neighbor. Jesus concluded: "There is no other commandment greater than these."

The scribes had been in conflict with Jesus since the beginning of his ministry; but this scribe agrees with Jesus and paraphrases Hosea 6:6, affirming that *love of God and neighbor are more important* than the laws concerning ritual sacrifices.

Jesus notes the wisdom of the man's response (v. 34), and tells him that he is not far from the Kingdom of God. Those who live by the love commandments will be able to enter into the life of God's Kingdom. With these words, Jesus' critics are silenced; and after this "no one dared" to ask Jesus any question.

In the reading from Hebrews 9, God's love is revealed through the priesthood of Jesus. As High Priest, Jesus entered once and for all into the Holy Place through the sacrifice of his own blood for our sake. This was far superior to the earlier sacrifices of animals' blood that brought only temporary relief from sin. Jesus was the pure one without blemish, who suffered on our behalf and offered himself through the eternal Spirit, enabling us to worship God with purified consciences.

In the Old Testament passage another manifestation of devotion to God and others is seen in the loyalty of Ruth to her mother-in-law during a famine in Judah. Naomi advises her daughters-in-law, Orpah and Ruth, to "go back each of you to your mother's house" (1:8) rather than remain with her. They are to leave with her love and prayers that they will find security with new husbands.

They are reluctant to part from her; but she reminds them that she can never be their mother-in-law again now that her sons are dead and she can no longer bear children. Finally, Orpah kisses Naomi and leaves; but Ruth clings to her, and in a moving speech declares her devotion (vv. 16-17).

Ruth's words are remarkable not only for the beauty of the language and the depth of her loyalty, but also for her declaration that: "Your people shall be my people, and your God my God." Ruth's love for Naomi leads her to renounce her family and her gods, and in a binding oath, she chooses to go as an alien and an unmarried woman to Judah.

When Naomi sees that Ruth is determined, she allows her to follow. Ruth and Naomi travel to Judah, where Ruth eventually marries and bears a son who will be the grandfather of King David.

Love of God and neighbor are the ways of life in the Kingdom of God. How can we follow the example of Jesus in our daily lives to love God with all our being? How do we then extend this love to others as well?

Proper 27

Adorn your house as you please; but do not forget those in distress. They are temples of far greater worth. —St. John Chrysostom.

In today's Gospel, Jesus warns his disciples to beware of the scribes, who call public attention to themselves through their privileged positions (Mk. 12:38-40). Scribes were a learned group trained in both law and Scripture, and were allied with the chief priests and elders opposing Jesus (2:16; 3:22; 9:14).

Because they were well versed in the law, they were able to use this to exploit others—"they devour widows' houses" (v. 40a). Moreover, their public display of piety with long prayers did not lead to justice for the needy.

They observe a poor widow, among the most vulnerable members of society—who symbolizes those exploited by the privileged classes. Jewish law demanded care for sojourners, orphans, and widows. Without inheritance rights, widows were dependent on other family members or charity.

Jesus sat and watched the crowd as individuals passed by and put money into the treasury. In Jesus' time, temples often functioned as banks; but here it is assumed that these were contributions for temple upkeep. The noise as coins fell into the large metal receptacles would call attention to the amount being donated. Many rich people put in large sums. In contrast, a poor widow contributed two copper pennies—the smallest coin in circulation.

Jesus explains: "Truly I tell you, this poor widow has put in more than all those who are contributing to the treasury" (v. 43). As with the widow of Zarephath in the Old Testament (1 Ki. 17:8-16), her contribution was truly sacrificial. Out of her poverty, she gave everything and put her very existence at risk. In contrast, what the rich—such as the scribes—gave did not much deplete their wealth.

Jesus does not explicitly praise the widow's actions in giving all. But his observation highlights the oppression of the poor by powerful people who ignore God's call for justice. Immediately following this incident, Jesus predicts the destruction of the temple (13:1-3), in which the whole repressive religious system will be destroyed.

The widow's gift of "everything she had" also foreshadows Jesus' coming sacrifice of his life: "though he was rich, yet for [our] sakes he became poor, so that by his poverty [we] might become rich" (2 Cor. 8:9).

The passage from Hebrews 9 continues the comparison of the ministry of the earthly high priests with the priesthood of Jesus. Jesus, as God's Messiah, gave of himself totally, once and for all, as the perfect sacrifice. He has gone to dwell in heaven, and now offers limitless intercessions on our behalf.

Jesus stands in contrast to the priests who repeatedly present the blood of animals for atonement. In contrast, Jesus brought once-for-all deliverance. Thus it is with joy that we await his coming again in glory to make our salvation complete.

In the Old Testament reading, a Moabite woman named Ruth had left her homeland to follow her Israelite mother-in-law, Naomi, back to Judah. Both women were widows, and Naomi acts to insure Ruth's future by helping her find a husband—Ruth's late husband's kinsman, Boaz. She attracts his attention after gathering grain in his fields, since Jewish law decreed that the edges of a field should be left for "the poor and the alien" to harvest (Lev. 19:9-10).

In due time, Ruth bears a son, who blesses Naomi in old age. This child, named Obed, was the grandfather of King David and is listed in the genealogies in Matthew 1:5 and Luke 3:32.

How are we called to honor God with the gifts we have been given? What does your own giving reveal about what you value?

Proper 28

God is eager to visit and invite brave spiritual explorers. ... Those who prefer that the ground always remain beneath their feet and that God remain predictable would be prudent to refrain from answering the door should God happen to knock.   —Edward Hays.

Apocalyptic literature is concerned with the end of human history. It is highly symbolic in its language, and is meant to provide encouragement to the faithful during times of trial.

The apocalyptic writers were successors to the prophets, who repeatedly warned of God's judgment and the coming Day of the Lord—when there would be a new creation, with justice for those God would preserve from the great final cataclysm.

Jesus began his ministry by proclaiming that "the time is fulfilled, and the kingdom of God has come near ... " (Mk. 1:15). Now, as his earthly ministry is coming to a close, Jesus addresses his disciples for the final time before his Passion.

Jesus' prediction of the destruction of the temple (13:1-8) is followed by warnings of persecution (vv. 9-13); and cosmic destruction (vv. 14-23) before the coming of the Son of Man (vv. 24-27). The discourse concludes with Jesus' parables and sayings to his followers about the necessity for vigilance (vv. 28-37).

Jesus had been teaching in the temple, and as he was leaving, one of the disciples expressed amazement at the size of the temple buildings. Jesus responded by declaring that the temple will be completely destroyed—not a stone will remain standing. Jesus' earlier action in the temple of overturning the corrupt moneychangers' tables was a symbolic act, warning of the coming destruction.

After the disciples ask what signs will precede these calamitous events, Jesus warns them to be cautious and to guard against false messiahs who will lead them astray. They should not be alarmed by talk of "wars and rumors of wars." Such predictions of conflict among nations, earthquakes, and famine were common in the Old Testament prophetic writings. All of this is seen as part of the Divine plan that will ultimately lead to greater revelation. Just as labor pains indicate that a child is about to be born, so do these events signal the coming of the Kingdom.

Hebrews also offers encouragement to the fledgling Christian community as they "see the Day approaching" (10:25): Christ has "offered for all time a single sacrifice for sins" (v. 12), and sits at "the right hand of God." Now Christ, who is both priest, and *at the same time* victim, has moved from the cross to the sanctuary of heaven itself, where he makes intercession for God's people. Therefore believers are to "provoke one another to love and good deeds" (v. 24) as they await the coming Day of the Lord.

In the Old Testament reading, hope for the future is realized as a barren woman's prayers for the gift of a child are answered. Childlessness in ancient Israel was regarded as a sign of God's displeasure. Thus when Hannah had not conceived a child, she went to the temple at Shiloh and prayed fervently for one, promising to dedicate her child to the Lord's service.

She was blessed with a boy that she named Samuel, meaning "I have asked him of the Lord" (1 Sam. 2:20). She took the weaned Samuel to the temple, where he remained in the service of the priest Eli until God called him to be the nation's prophet, to guide Israel through many difficult times.

Today's readings call attention to perseverance in faith and hope for the future. As you reflect on trying events in your life and in the world today, what are the signs that God is present? How do you find hope and inspiration in difficult times? What new things can you expect to be born out of seeming disaster?

Proper 29

Jesus is king precisely because he has come to bear witness to the truth. —Karl Rahner.

The institution of the monarchy came relatively late in Israel's history. Whereas other kings were often regarded as gods, the Lord God was the only sovereign of Israel (Jer. 10:7-10; Ps. 95:3). Honoring the covenant between God and Israel also distinguished Israel from other nations. A king was often called the "anointed one" (1 Sam. 2:35), from which "messiah" was derived.

David, greatest of all of Israel's kings, was the one through whom the Messiah would come. Today we read David's last words, contrasting just and wicked rulers. David himself is described as "anointed of the God of Jacob, the favorite of the Strong One of Israel" (2 Sam. 23:1).

The Gospels frequently applied royal imagery to Jesus, as when the Magi ask, "Where is the child who has been born king of the Jews?" (Mt. 2:2). Matthew's genealogy established that Jesus was of the royal Davidic lineage. Although Jesus was accused of royal pretensions (Lk. 23:2), he resisted all efforts to make him king (Jn. 6:15). Yet when Jesus entered Jerusalem, the crowd proclaimed, "Blessed is the king who comes in the name of the Lord!"

The Gospel reading for this Christ the King Sunday is from John's account of Jesus' trial before Pontius Pilate, with the royal status of Jesus being key to the interrogation. A beaten and scorned Jesus hardly seems kingly. He had been flogged, dressed in a purple robe with a crown of thorns, and mocked by the soldiers: "Hail, King of the Jews!" (Jn. 19:3).

Pilate asks Jesus: "Are you the King of the Jews?" (18:33). Jesus had already been found guilty by the Jewish authorities, and now Pilate sought to verify the vague charges. Jesus here neither affirms nor denies the accusation.

In verse 36, Jesus defines the sense in which he is indeed a king: "My kingdom is not from this world." If the Kingdom that Jesus proclaimed belonged in any sense to the temporal world, he would not have been handed over without a fight from his followers.

Pilate once again asks Jesus, "So are you a king?" Jesus then replies that he has come into the world to bring a reign of truth. Those to whom truth matters will heed his word. In him, the world can identify the nature of God most fully.

Jesus exemplifies the character of true kingship and redefines worldly assumptions about power. In him there is no personal vanity; and he makes no demands at others' expense. He came to serve and not to be served. His Kingdom creates a new community of believers who hear and obey his voice. This is the essential meaning of our proclaiming *Christ as King.*

The description of the exalted Christ in Revelation provides a vision of the celestial Kingdom. Addressing the seven churches, the writer begins with blessings of peace. The source of worship is the Divine One, the victor, accompanied by seven spirits or archangels who serve God and Jesus (1:4).

The triumphant and exalted Christ of the vision is described as the faithful witness. He is the first from among the dead in his victorious Resurrection—ruler of the kings of the earth. By his love we are freed from sin through his blood. As Christ's redeemed, we are ourselves a kingdom and priests to God the Father.

The Lord God is Alpha and Omega—first and last—the One "who is and who was and who is to come, the Almighty."

What are the defining characteristics of the Kingdom that Jesus proclaims? In what ways do you see evidence of this Kingdom in the world today? What is our role as individuals in bringing the Kingdom of God to reality?

Lectionary Readings

Advent 1: Isaiah 64:1-9; Psalm 80:1-7, 16-18; 1 Corinthians 1:3-9; Mark 13:24-37

Advent 2: Isaiah 40:1-11; Psalm 85:1-2, 8-13; 2 Peter 3:8-15a; Mark 1:1-8

Advent 3: Isaiah 61:1-4, 8-11; Psalm 126 or Canticle 3; 1 Thessalonians 5:16-24; John 1:6-8, 19-28

Advent 4: 2 Samuel 7:1-11, 16; Psalm 89:1-4, 19-26 or Canticle 3; Romans 16:25-27; Luke 1:26-38

Christmas Day: Isaiah 9:2-7; Psalm 96; Titus 2:11-14; Luke 2:1-14 (15-20)

Christmas 1: Isaiah 61:10–62:3; Psalm 147 or 147:13-21; Galatians 3:23-25; 4:4-7; John 1:1-18

Holy Name: Numbers 6:22-27; Psalm 8; Galatians 4:4-7 or Philippians 2:5-11; Luke 2:15-21

Christmas 2: Jeremiah 31:7-14; Psalm 84 or 84:1-8; Ephesians 1:3-6, 15-19a; Matthew 2:13-15, 19-23 or Luke 2:41-52 or Matthew 2:1-12

The Epiphany: Isaiah 60:1-6; Psalm 72:1-7, 10-14; Ephesians 3:1-12; Matthew 2:1-12

Epiphany 1: Genesis 1:1-5; Psalm 29; Acts 19:1-7; Mark 1:4-11

Epiphany 2: 1 Samuel 3:1-10 (11-20); Psalm 139:1-5, 12-17; 1 Corinthians 6:12-20; John 1:43-51

Epiphany 3: Jonah 3:1-5, 10; Psalm 62:6-14; 1 Corinthians 7:29-31; Mark 1:14-20

The Presentation: Malachi 3:1-4; Psalm 84 or Psalm 24:7-10; Hebrews 2:14-18; Luke 2:22-40

Epiphany 4: Deuteronomy 18:15-20; Psalm 111; 1 Corinthians 8:1-13; Mark 1:21-28

Epiphany 5: Isaiah 40:21-31; Psalm 147:1-12, 21c; 1 Corinthians 9:16-23; Mark 1:29-39

Epiphany 6: 2 Kings 5:1-14; Psalm 30; 1 Corinthians 9:24-27; Mark 1:40-45

Epiphany 7: Isaiah 43:18-25; Psalm 41; 2 Corinthians 1:18-22; Mark 2:1-12

Epiphany 8: Hosea 2:14-20; Psalm 103:1-13, 22; 2 Corinthians 3:1-6; Mark 2:13-22

Last Epiphany: 2 Kings 2:1-12; Psalm 50:1-6; 2 Corinthians 4:3-6; Mark 9:2-9

Ash Wednesday: Joel 2:1-2, 12-17; Psalm 103 or 103:8-14; 2 Corinthians 5:20b–6:10; Matthew 6:1-6, 16-21

Lent 1: Genesis 9:8-17; Psalm 25:1-9; 1 Peter 3:18-22; Mark 1:9-15

Lent 2: Genesis 17:1-7, 15-16; Psalm 22:22-30; Romans 4:13-25; Mark 8:31-38

Lent 3: Exodus 20:1-17; Psalm 19; 1 Corinthians 1:18-25; John 2:13-22

Lent 4: Numbers 21:4-9; Psalm 107:1-3, 17-22; Ephesians 2:1-10; John 3:14-21

Lent 5: Jeremiah 31:31-34; Psalm 51:1-13; Hebrews 5:5-10; John 12:20-33

Palm Sunday: Isaiah 50:4-9a; Psalm 31:9-16; Philippians 2:5-11; Mark 14:1–15:47

Maundy Thursday: Exodus 12:1-4 (5-10), 11-14; Psalm 116:1, 10-17; 1 Corinthians 11:23-26; John 13:1-17, 31b-35

Good Friday: Isaiah 52:13–53:12; Psalm 22; Hebrews 10:16-25; John 18:1–19:42

Easter Day: Acts 10:34-43; Psalm 118:1-2, 14-24; 1 Corinthians 15:1-11; John 20:1-18 or Mark 16:1-8

Easter 2: Acts 4:32-35; Psalm 133; 1 John 1:1–2:2; John 20:19-31

Easter 3: Acts 3:12-19; Psalm 4; 1 John 3:1-7; Luke 24:36b-48

Easter 4: Acts 4:5-12; Psalm 23; 1 John 3:16-24; John 10:11-18

Easter 5: Acts 8:26-40; Psalm 22:24-30; 1 John 4:7-21; John 15:1-8

Easter 6: Acts 10:44-48; Psalm 98; 1 John 5:1-6; John 15:9-17

Ascension Day: Acts 1:1-11; Psalm 47; Ephesians 1:15-23; Luke 24:44-53

Easter 7: Acts 1:15-17, 21-26; Psalm 1; 1 John 5:9-13; John 17:6-19

Day of Pentecost: Acts 2:1-21; Psalm 104:25-35, 37b; Romans 8:22-27; John 15:26-27; 16:4b-15

Trinity Sunday: Isaiah 6:1-8; Psalm 29 or Canticle 2 or 13; Romans 8:12-17; John 3:1-17

Proper 1: 2 Kings 5:1-14; Psalm 30; 1 Corinthians 9:24-27; Mark 1:40-45

Proper 2: Isaiah 43:18-25; Psalm 41; 2 Corinthians 1:18-22; Mark 2:1-12

Proper 3: Hosea 2:14-20; Psalm 103:1-13, 22; 2 Corinthians 3:1-6; Mark 2:13-22

Proper 4: 1 Samuel 3:1-10 (11-20); Psalm 139:1-5, 12-17; 2 Corinthians 4:5-12; Mark 2:23–3:6

Proper 5: 1 Samuel 8:4-11 (12-15), 16-20 (11:14-15); Psalm 138; 2 Corinthians 4:13–5:1; Mark 3:20-35

Proper 6: 1 Samuel 15:34–16:13; Psalm 20; 2 Corinthians 5:6-10 (11-13), 14-17; Mark 4:26-34

Proper 7: 1 Samuel 17:(1a, 4-11, 19-23), 32-49; Psalm 9:9-20; 2 Corinthians 6:1-13; Mark 4:35-41

Proper 8: 2 Samuel 1:1, 17-27; Psalm 130; 2 Corinthians 8:7-15; Mark 5:21-43

Proper 9: 2 Samuel 5:1-5, 9-10; Psalm 48; 2 Corinthians 12:2-10; Mark 6:1-13

Proper 10: 2 Samuel 6:1-5, 12b-19; Psalm 24; Ephesians 1:3-14; Mark 6:14-29

Proper 11: 2 Samuel 7:1-14a; Psalm 89:20-37; Ephesians 2:11-22; Mark 6:30-34, 53-56

Proper 12: 2 Samuel 11:1-15; Psalm 14; Ephesians 3:14-21; John 6:1-21

Proper 13: 2 Samuel 11:26–12:13a; Psalm 51:1-13; Ephesians 4:1-16; John 6:24-35

The Transfiguration: Exodus 34:29-35; Psalm 99; 2 Peter 1:13-21; Luke 9:28-36

Proper 14: 2 Samuel 18:5-9, 15, 31-33; Psalm 130; Ephesians 4:25–5:2; John 6:35, 41-51

Proper 15: 1 Kings 2:10-12; 3:3-14; Psalm 111; Ephesians 5:15-20; John 6:51-58

Proper 16: 1 Kings 8:(1, 6, 10-11), 22-30, 41-43; Psalm 84; Ephesians 6:10-20; John 6:56-69

Proper 17: Song of Solomon 2:8-13; Psalm 45:1-2, 7-10; James 1:17-27; Mark 7:1-8, 14-15, 21-23

Proper 18: Proverbs 22:1-2, 8-9, 22-23; Psalm 125; James 2:1-10 (11-13), 14-17; Mark 7:24-37

Proper 19: Proverbs 1:20-33; Psalm 19; James 3:1-12; Mark 8:27-38

Proper 20: Proverbs 31:10-31; Psalm 1; James 3:13–4:3, 7-8a; Mark 9:30-37

Proper 21: Esther 7:1-6, 9-10; 9:20-22; Psalm 124; James 5:13-20; Mark 9:38-50

Proper 22: Job 1:1; 2:1-10; Psalm 26; Hebrews 1:1-4; 2:5-12; Mark 10:2-16

Proper 23: Job 23:1-9, 16-17; Psalm 22:1-15; Hebrews 4:12-16; Mark 10:17-31

Proper 24: Job 38:1-7 (34-41); Psalm 104:1-9, 25, 37c; Hebrews 5:1-10; Mark 10:35-45

Proper 25: Job 42:1-6, 10-17; Psalm 34:1-8 (19-22); Hebrews 7:23-28; Mark 10:46-52

All Saints' Day: Isaiah 25:6-9 or Wisdom of Solomon 3:1-9; Psalm 24; Revelation 21:1-6a; John 11:32-44

Proper 26: Ruth 1:1-18; Psalm 146; Hebrews 9:11-14; Mark 12:28-34

Proper 27: Ruth 3:1-5; 4:13-17; Psalm 127; Hebrews 9:24-28; Mark 12:38-44

Proper 28: 1 Samuel 1:4-20; 1 Samuel 2:1-10 (Song of Hanna); Hebrews 10:11-14 (15-18), 19-25; Mark 13:1-8

Proper 29: 2 Samuel 23:1-7; Psalm 132:1-13 (14-19); Revelation 1:4b-8; John 18:33-37

Made in the USA
Monee, IL
14 October 2020